"With a style both learned and witty, Petrotta ranges through the biblical canon, illuminating from a surprising angle texts that are often overlooked or dismissed. He shows that an expanded notion of humor is vital for probing exegesis, that biblical humor is itself a mode of theological reflection. This is serious scholarship of the most pleasurable kind, suitable for a wide audience of scholars, students, and readers, both Jews and Christians."

—ELLEN F. DAVIS, Amos Ragan Kearns Distinguished Professor of Bible and Practical Theology, Duke Divinity School

"Anthony J. Petrotta's elegant examination of the structure and function of humor in the Bible combines the accumulated knowledge of a professor, the practical wisdom of a pastor, and the mature faith of a lifelong disciple. *God at the Improv* deftly balances erudite analyses by Kierkegaard and Niebuhr with pithy witticisms from Woody Allen and Chuck Jones. Exhibiting both careful scholarship and a sanctified imagination, this book achieves the twin goals of all successful writing: it delights even as it instructs."

—DAVID DENNY, author of *Man Overboard* and *Some Divine Commotion*

"I always felt Luke was the funniest writer in the Bible. Eutychus means 'lucky.' But Dr. Petrotta has opened my eyes to the extent and depth of humor in Scripture. Humor is the capacity to discover and express the absurd; this becomes all the more clear when the status quo is backlit by God's kingdom. We should laugh at whatever culture props up as god."

—JOHN DELHOUSAYE, Professor of New Testament and Spiritual Formation, Phoenix Seminary

"Tony's serious scholarly understandings are livened by his sense of humor—a welcome surprise that will keep readers smiling as they learn."

—SHARON GALLAGHER, Editor, *Radix* magazine

"Anthony Petrotta's latest work, *God at the Improv*, offers a delightfully refreshing and intellectually challenging contextualization of humor via the lens of Scripture. While Petrotta's keen eye for uncovering instances of humor functioning as a rhetorical feature of the text is both laudable and impressive, it is his implicit invitation for us to consider a sense of humor among God's immutable characteristics that sets this book apart."

—TIMOTHY GARNER, Associate Vice President for Institutional Analytics and Professor of Sociology, Franklin College

"For me, the best part of humor is the surprise. 'I didn't expect that!' That twist brings a smile, a twinkle, a laugh. In this delightful book, Tony Petrotta shows us that the God of the Bible is full of surprises: with Sarah, Jonah, Elijah, Jesus, and more. Whenever God steps in, our mouths are filled with laughter, and our tongues with songs of joy (Ps 126). This book gives us a playful, slanted glimpse at biblical truth, and leaves us with a sense of awe and a smile."

—KURT FREDRICKSON, Associate Dean for Professional Doctoral Programs, Associate Professor of Pastoral Ministry, Fuller Theological Seminary

"Many people find the idea of humor in the Bible unacceptable. Salvation is serious business, they say, and there is no place here for the frivolous and playful. Petrotta shows us another way. Gently, firmly, delightfully, he shows that the Scripture is full of humor. From the laughter of Sarah to the repartee of the Syrophoenician woman humor is everywhere in the Bible. This book will make you think . . . and imagine. Above all, it will make you laugh."

—DR. PETER R. ROGERS, Director of the Center for Bible Study and Vicar of St. Andrews Episcopal Church, Antelope, CA

"Petrotta's readings revel in Scripture's comic rhetoric as being inherent to its transformative purpose. He shows us both how to read and how to live. The Bible's humor in his framing embraces an array of tropes and literary strategies that guide the trusting reader toward authentic life under God, whose grace is essentially comic without negating tragic reality. These readings show how humor anticipates faith, requiring much the same dispositions."

—BRUCE HANSEN, Senior Staff Specialist, InterVarsity Christian Fellowship

God at the Improv

God at the Improv

Humor and the Holy in Scripture

Anthony J. Petrotta

FOREWORD BY David W. Gill

CASCADE *Books* · Eugene, Oregon

GOD AT THE IMPROV
Humor and the Holy in Scripture

Cascade Books
An Imprint of Wipf and Stock Publishers
199 W. 8th Ave., Suite 3
Eugene, OR 97401

www.wipfandstock.com

PAPERBACK ISBN: 978-1-5326-9081-5
HARDCOVER ISBN: 978-1-5326-9082-2
EBOOK ISBN: 978-1-5326-9083-9

Cataloguing-in-Publication data:

Names: Petrotta, Anthony J.
Title: God at the Improv : humor and the holy in scripture / Anthony J. Petrotta.
Description: Eugene, OR: Cascade Books, 2020 | Includes bibliographical references.
Identifiers: ISBN 978-1-5326-9081-5 (paperback) | ISBN 978-1-5326-9082-2 (hardcover) | ISBN 978-1-5326-9083-9 (ebook)
Subjects: LCSH: Wit and humor—Religious aspects—Christianity. | Wit and humor in the Bible. | Laughter—Religious aspects—Christianity.
Classification: BV4647.J68 P55 2020 (print) | BV4647 (ebook)

Scripture quotations, unless otherwise noted are from the *New Revised Standard Version of the Bible*, copyright 1989.

The poem "Parable of the Potter" is used by permission of David Denny from his book of poems, *Man Overboard: A Tale of Divine Compassion*, Eugene, Wipf & Stock, 2013, copyrighted 2013.

Dedication

Pamela, my sparkle

Nana and Jack, great laughers

Avalyn, Khaellum, Cameron, and Eleanor,
may the Lord make his face to shine upon you

Table of Contents

Foreword

By David W. Gill

My earliest recollections of humor in the Bible were as a kid laughing about the "shortest man in the Bible"—"Bildad the Shuhite" (not Zacchaeus the diminutive tax collector). And the first mention of tennis in the Bible: "and Joseph served in Pharaoh's court." Of course, we juveniles snickered whenever we read the verses pertaining to "pissing against the wall" (e.g., 1 Sam 25:22, KJV). Otherwise, the Bible was serious business full of dire warnings and demanding rules.

Sometime in my twenties, without looking for it, I began to discover some real humor in the Bible. The Broadway play *Godspell* brilliantly illuminated the humor of Jesus' parables. Some New Testament scholar helped me see the humor on the Day of Pentecost when, after some ecstatic tongue-speaking made onlookers accuse the Christians of being drunk, Peter quipped, "They can't possibly be drunk! It's only nine o'clock in the morning!" (Acts 2:15). I thought, what a great way to get a big laugh, relax a potentially hostile crowd, and imply that these are just ordinary guys who might be in the pub later after work. Peter's humble humor set the mood for a careful listening to the gospel and a mass of conversions.

Humor is normally the result of a kind of incongruity. A line of thought or action suddenly veers off in an unexpected, even comic, direction. I can imagine laughter after the resurrection when the disciples were suddenly struck at the novelty of a dead man rising—and their weak movement breaking the laws of nature and expectations of society. It's kind of like the laughter of the victors after a huge sports upset. Humor is often about the unexpected, even the absurd and transgressive.

Much humor involves a jesting and caricaturing of ourselves and others. For example:

> A Swede and his son went out for some ice fishing. After several hours they had caught nothing so the Swede said to his son, "Go over there to those Norwegians and ask them how they are catching so many fish while we have caught nothing." The little boy went over and came back: "Dad, they cut a hole in the ice."

I am sure the story has been told with the identities flipped. Harmless, humorous, part of how neighbors can joke with each other and laugh. But it takes some real sensitivity and discretion to know where to draw the line beyond which is cruelty. Humor becomes toxic when it involves the mocking of the weak by the strong, like the derision experienced by Jesus when, after his arrest, he was crowned with thorns, mocked, and beaten. It is sick, not humorous, when leaders mock and insult others.

But humor is often a blessing. Self-effacing humor has great power in communication. Several years ago relations between the USA and France were a bit frayed. A USA leader even urged that Americans rename french fries as "freedom fries" (not everyone in France appreciated this). As I stood up to give a lecture at a conference in France during those years, I began, "I am honored to be here. As requested I will attempt to give my lecture in my imperfect French. But I will only do so if you agree to correct me and my mistakes—and you know how we Americans love to be corrected by the French!" A roar of laughter and they were on my side from that point on.

The great Danish philosopher and Christian Søren Kierkegaard (1813–1855) was both the source and recipient of biting, sometimes caustic, humor and criticism. He devoted many pages of his major work *Concluding Unscientific Postscript* (1846) to reflections on humor and the role of the comic and the jest, especially in relation to suffering and religious faith. There is a dialectic (an interplay of opposites) between suffering and humor, and between the serious and the comic. Humor operates in the boundary zone between the ethical life (following the rules) and the religious life (following the living God moment-by-moment). I think what Kierkegaard was saying was that as we draw near to the Living Holy God we see the absurdity (and wonder) of our own weakness and finitude being received by God. Who am I that you should love me?

From juvenile Bible jokes to five-hundred-page treatises by philosophers, humor is an inextricable part of life, even if some of a more puritanical bent may have wished otherwise. And how blessed we are now to have a guide to show us the biblical foundations of an understanding and appreciation of humor. Rev. Dr. Anthony Petrotta (always "Tony" to me) was the smartest student (of forty) in my seminary course "Theology and Ethics of Jacques Ellul" back in fall 1976. I have followed his life and career closely for over forty years as he became a recognized and appreciated biblical scholar, a true doctor in the church. And I have watched him obey his call to the priesthood and pastorate. I have read his research and visited his parishes. What he has provided in this book is the product of this balance of solid scholarship and a real engagement in the lives of the people.

We live in a world of deeply serious challenges and threats. The daily news can weigh heavily upon us. We need to learn how to "lighten up" and see the humorous and comical in the midst of the serious. We also live in an age of mocking and cruel attempts at humor from political leaders down to social media attackers. This is not funny or tolerable but the answer is not just to suppress the evil but to rediscover the good when it comes to humor. That is the gift awaiting readers of this book.

David W. Gill (www.davidwgill.org) recently retired from a forty-year career as university, business school, and seminary professor of Christian ethics and business ethics. He is now a writer working on his tenth book. He serves as part-time, volunteer "workplace discipleship coach" at First Covenant Church, Oakland, California.

Acknowledgments

Mount Angel Abbey Guesthouse and Retreat Center has been a source of peace and study for nearly two decades. The staff at the center, the bookstore, and library are always gracious, and attending the compline service with the monks in the chapel is a lovely way to end a day of study. Sister Rebecca with the Benedictine Sisters graciously found me a room when the Abbey Guesthouse was being renovated. The love of the Lord shines on her face always. Candace Duncan and Leslie Hurd were wizards with the formatting.

Bill Zuelke, my spiritual director, always managed to pull me back to the center as I fretted over the making of this book and as I grew into being the priest at St. Francis Episcopal Church (Wilsonville, Oregon). The parishioners of St. Francis were also gracious and well-meaning with their "Is the book done yet?" questions. Walt and Marija Kuzmen gave a gracious gift to St. Francis Church to assist me with the costs involved in the study, writing, and the publication of the book.

I wish to thank Dave Denny for permission to use the poem "Parable of the Potter," from his book *Man Overboard: A Tale of Divine Compassion*. These poems are both winsome and insightful.

Numerous colleagues and friends read portions of the book and offered good advice along the way. However, pride of place goes to Rev. Nancy Duff. She came to me first as a student when I taught at Fuller Seminary, Northern California. After I got ordained, she became a helpful colleague. She was my most critical and gracious reader along the way. I don't know how many times she said, "Nice line—you can cut it." Why would I cut it if it's such a nice line? Because her comments always made *Improv* a better book. Thanks are inadequate to say for what she's done to help, gently chide, and encourage me over the years. *Todah rabah*, Nancy.

List of Abbreviations

ESV	English Standard Version
JPS	Jewish Publication Society
KJV	King James Version
NRSV	New Revised Standard Version
OED	Oxford English Dictionary
RSV	Revised Standard Version

Introduction

> Humor should be a feature of the in-breaking kingdom. It is to
> inspire that sense of wonder and joy, that playful, spirited sense
> of possibility, and to inspire those practices that flow from it and
> renew it. . . .
>
> —SAMUEL WELLS,
> *IMPROVISATION: THE DRAMA OF CHRISTIAN ETHICS*, 15

Everyone laughs. Either for, with, or—unfortunately—*at* someone. Everyone laughs and the sharing of humor with others is one of the supreme joys of life and friendships. Laughter itself, though, is many-sided. Tendentious people rarely laugh *with* you, but they've been known to give wry smiles occasionally. Ornery people are singularly unable to create humor, but they are often fun to watch—from a distance. Petulant people have a hard time finding humor. Polite people will give nervous laughter, not entirely sure it is polite to laugh at someone. Incredulous people will laugh, often joyfully, when the not-believed unfolds before them. Sadly, in our broken world, some people have been so wronged that their laughter lies buried in places where God alone sits with them.

We all laugh and do so for various reasons and on sundry occasions. Young boys seem to revel in "potty humor." Teenagers tend towards a more sarcastic humor as they find their way towards acceptance and adulthood. Bosses often tell jokes, though I'm hard pressed to say that they are truly funny. I suspect it is a good discipline that most of us have learned to feign laughter on occasion.

Everyone laughs—yet we seldom ask *why* we laugh or *what circumstances* afford occasions for laughter.

My initial foray into humor and Scripture came studying wordplay in the book of Micah. A book by M. M. Mahood, *Shakespeare's Wordplay*, gave me the framework to move beyond the simple observation of Micah's wordplays as mere sound-play. Most scholars note the aural plays but fail to address why and for what purposes Micah uses wordplays to deliver his message. Hardly anyone mentions the possibility of humor.

Mahood observes the various uses of wordplay in Shakespeare beyond the obvious ornamental flourish. In particular she identifies the wit Shakespeare employs in his use of wordplays. Micah similarly uses wordplay in diverse ways to call his people to see things differently.

It seems that the whys and wherefores of humor are as diverse as the types of laughter we experience, from smirks and wry smiles to guffaws and belly laughs.

*

"Only a fool, or one of those who believe in theories would presume
to say in general, what the purpose of joking is . . . Every general
theory of jokes known to me is wrong."

—TED COHEN, *JOKES*, 9, 43

Everyone laughs but we don't always laugh for the same reasons or occasions. Tickling is torture to some people. "Put-downs" are funnier to the instigator than the fall guy.

Humor—if funny—will always have a point of some sort. Thus, one of the oldest and dearest theories of humor (Aristotle's) maintains that humor entails a sense of *superiority*. I first encountered a Superiority Theory of humor years ago while reading a science fiction novel (my untrustworthy memory says it was by Robert Heinlein). The comment was to the effect that all humor is "put down."

Scorn, derision, sarcasm, and the sneer and *fleering frump* are part of humor's repertoire. Nearly all theories of humor recognize this dark side. There is a Greek term that names this less-than-endearing side of humor: *phthonic* (it comes to personify envy, jealousy, and malice in Greek thought). Humor often has a sting to it.

This Superiority Theory highlights that humor is not wholly innocent. There is, as philosopher Thomas Hobbes says, a "sudden glory" experienced by those who are not the object of the humor. Much humor seeks to expose faulty thinking and actions. Marie Collins Swabey observes, "Undeniably, a chief function of laughter is to help sweep the world free of shams, superstitions, outworn customs, and false beliefs, a process which leaves us with a chill sense of fewer supports to lean on."[1]

Kids in a school playground learn this mischievous side of humor early, sometimes indelibly. I have always suspected that when a baby giggles she is thinking something like, "What is this codger doing making such goofy faces . . ." More particularly, we rarely enjoy our cherished beliefs being called into question with a laugh or a joke.

Any appeal to "I was only *joking*" seldom eases a humorous situation gone awry.

Even if we accept that humor is not wholly innocent, the most obvious association with humor is laughter. Humor elicits some *physical* reaction. Herbert Spenser (nineteenth-century philosopher and biologist) brought out the obvious fact that there is a "muscular release" (laughter) from built up energy in response to a given (humorous) situation. Henri Bergson and Sigmund Freud (both twentieth century) followed and developed this component of humor, dubbed the Relief Theory of Humor.

A fair question to ask is, what situations might bring about this muscular release, especially given the *sting* of humor? Kant (nineteenth century) argues that laughter is the response to a perceived incongruity, be it in words or actions. Hence the Incongruity Theory is yet a third general way of viewing humor. William Hazlitt (nineteenth-century literary critic and essayist) expressed it this way: "Man is the only animal that laughs and weeps; for he is the only

> *Vladimir Propp quotes Yurenov (a Russian film historian who attempted a list of different kinds of laughter), "Laughter can be joyful and sad, kind and irate, clever and silly, proud and warm-hearted, indulgent and fawning, contemptuous and sacred, offensive and encouraging, impudent and shy, friendly and hostile, ironic and ingenuous, sarcastic and naïve, tender and rough, significant and groundless, triumphant and justificatory, shameless and confused. The list can be extended: cheerful, mournful, nervous, hysterical, humiliating, physiological, bestial. There can even be melancholy laughter!"[2]*

---

1. Swabey, *Comic Laughter*, 247.

2. Propp, *On the Comic*, 11. A search of the Internet yielded nearly five hundred thousand titles for books and articles on humor and over one hundred thousand titles on laughter.

animal that is struck with the difference between what things are, and what they ought to be."[3]

No theory covers all the contingent functions, forms, and experiences of this universal trait of shared humanity. Even if we can't agree on a single theory of humor, we still find ourselves snickering, chuckling, snorting, chortling, and even cachinnating at some*thing*!

*

Laughter is indeed a very good counterpoise to the spleen, and it seems but reasonable that we should be capable of receiving joy from what is no real good to us, since we can receive grief from what is no real evil.

—JOSEPH ADDISON,
ESSAYS IN CRITICISM AND LITERARY THEORY, 26

Everyone laughs. Laughter, however, is not inevitable. Humor has been called a *luxury reflex*. In theory we could live our whole lives without laughter. Given a few days without food or water, however, we begin to wither—or get grouchy.

Laughter is not inevitable, though we live in a world of apparent inevitabilities. Surveys, data, and the "right side of history" seem to govern existence. And yet in this world of data and outcomes, surprisingly incongruous moments arrive that lift the burden of necessity with the "weight of glory" (2 Cor 4:17). Even the best data has a margin of error factored in. Humor testifies to the *necessity of contingency* in our lives. Humor turns on that moment when the tale or joke swerves to a side-road not seen at the start but seems, once taken, to be the more fitting path.

Humor attests to these surprises in our lives. In the movie *Mr. Saturday Night*, Billy Crystal plays an aging stand-up comedian reflecting on his life. I recall a refrain as he tells jokes to his brother and asks, "Did you see it coming?"[4] When we see a punch line coming, we seldom laugh. At best we give an amused smile, often out of courtesy.

In Matthew Jesus catches his audience, the Pharisees, off guard, "You strain at a gnat and swallow a camel" (Matt 23:24). It is a biting comment on the inconsistency of their actions. The combination of vivid image and

---

3. Morreal, *Philosophy of Laughter*, 65.

4. *Mr. Saturday Night*, 1992, directed by Billy Crystal; written by Lowell Ganz, Billy Crystal, and Babaloo Mandell.

apt analogy requires some response. If I were in the crowd that day, I may well have laughed—and then tried to pass it off as a cough if the leaders looked my way.

We should also note that Jesus' words in Matt 23:24 come as the third in a series of "woes." Humor often follows a series of items, usually three. "A prophet, a priest, and a prostitute walk into a bar . . ." The prophet and the priest will act predictably, as *professionally* religious people often do. The prostitute will act out of character, being in some fashion more *religious* than the prophet and the priest. She will break the pattern with a surprising word or action, yet one markedly appropriate to the occasion. The prophet and priest will not laugh, but anyone else there would likely snigger, at the very least.

Walter Nash gives a general framework for recognizing how humor works in texts.[5] He notes there is a *locus* (a word, phrase, image) that turns what could be a rather bland sentence into what we call a joke, or statement with a humorous intent. When we do not *see it coming,* and then we do see it, we laugh. The *surprise* allows us to catch sight of what we had not seen a moment ago.

Issues of form, structure, and purpose play their unique part in humor. Humor is neither innocent nor easily analyzed. It will be *surprising, incongruous* but also *apt* for the occasion, *biting* (though not devastating), and seeks to *amend,* not to condemn. The goal is to laugh, not cry (though even that is not universal since we have *tears of laughter* on occasion).

C. S. Lewis, in *Screwtape Letters,* seems to make the case that the enemy of humor is not so much seriousness as triviality.[6] Humor is that child in "The Emperor's New Clothes" who simply has to point out that the emperor has no clothes on! In literary language, humor plays an important *rhetorical* function: humor invites scrutiny of our assumptions and practices, as individuals and as a society. It not only amuses us but seeks to move us.

*

> "You told me a hundred times, Uncle Willie.
> Words with a 'k' in it are funny."
>
> —BEN CLARK, IN *THE SUNSHINE BOYS*

5. Nash, *Humour,* 1–12.

6. Lewis, *Screwtape.*

Theories may shed some light on humor, but I'm hard-pressed to say that a theory can generate humor. Similarly, examining the forms of humor, like the series of threes noted above, will not amuse us, I suspect. Indeed, examining how and why humor works often squelches it. More than one critic has noted that explaining humor is like dissecting frogs—they both inevitably die when cut apart.

Nash shows how humor plays out in the language used, the stylistic choices, and the social and cultural assumptions. The words, the material facts, and the logic combine into something that evokes laughter—or not! Comic discourse has a *location in society, a type of human interaction,* and *words or gestures* that might signal humorous intent.

For us to get the humorous side of Jesus' comments above, it helps to know that the religious authorities were, well, *religiously* religious. They were also, sometimes, out of touch with the person in the pew, as it were. Furthermore, prophets in ancient Israel were known for their direct and often caustic statements. What triggers the laughter is the image of a person swallowing a large object (a camel) but choking on a small object (a gnat). It is the incongruity between the beliefs and the actions that strike us as comic.

Jesus invites his audience, leaders included, to consider their outwardly pious actions as more show than substance. The rhetorical function is to change something—about the situation, ourselves, our culture, maybe even the world. Humor is an invitation to see differently; it becomes an "Adjustment Opportunity." Jesus' aim is to create change not scourge the leaders.

I feel confident that the religious leaders of Jesus' day did not laugh. To them Jesus was not being witty or clever. I'm equally confident, however, that those living under the burden of their leadership quite likely told this encounter to family and friends—and everybody laughed.

*

And the more I considered Christianity, the more I found that while
it had established a rule and an order, the chief aim of that order
was to give room for good things to run wild.

—G. K. CHESTERTON, *COLLECTED WORKS,* 1:300

Everyone laughs—because it is inevitable that we cannot anticipate all the contingencies of life.

My exploration of humor as a topic to take seriously continued over the years, and I gained confidence that humor might shed further light on particular passages in Scripture. It was again my general reading that led me to hone my questioning, broadening and enriching my readings of Scripture. Two books in particular stand out: the novel *Mazel* by Rebecca Goldstein and *Improvisation: The Drama of Christian Ethics* by Samuel Wells.

Mazel dramatizes whether fate or luck governs our lives. *Mazel tov* is an expression used to congratulate someone on a fortuitous happening in life or to wish someone well. Wells's *Improvisation* is a call to utilize skills that draw upon improvisational strategies to make decisions and carry out actions in our lives where single, inevitable responses may close off other possibilities and outcomes.

Mazel reflects on this contingent force that is the "imp of metaphysics."[7] *Mazel* is the "great confounder of closed systems and their pretenders"; it is the "saboteur of cosmic coziness."[8] Surprises often disrupt our plans or play havoc with our established beliefs.

Goldstein recounts a story that the only time the Jews in the *shtetel* ventured forth outside their safe self-imposed walls was during *Rosh Hashanah*, the High Holy Days in Jewish worship. They chanced forth for the ritual of *tashlich*, the casting (of sins). The rabbis, of course, instructed the Jews to "avert their gaze" and resist the "pull of alien enchantments."[9] Goldstein draws a wonderful picture of this occasion of venturing forth: "Perhaps precisely because *tashlich* [the casting away of sins] was so out of the ordinary, performed in the wildness beyond four walls, it was a great favorite among the children, inducing, despite its penitential purpose, *a rambunctiousness of high adventure.*"[10]

This ritual of repentance becomes a time of "rambunctiousness," a *mazel* time. The weight of the sins lifted and the normal necessity of being apart from the Gypsies who roamed outside the *shtetel* were suspended. Part of the ritual of repentance was to throw pieces of stale bread on the waters and watch the bread flow—always downstream. Goldstein says they had "more bread . . . than there had been sins committed this year by all the

---

7. Goldstein, *Mazel*, 5.

8. Goldstein, *Mazel*, 5, 34.

9. Goldstein, *Mazel*, 98.

10. Goldstein, *Mazel*, 99 (emphasis added).

Jews . . . in Galacia and even beyond."[11] The overabundance of bread is the contingent necessity in that world of indispensable obligation of repentance.

Is there enough bread for our sins? One mother in Goldstein's telling of this story explains to her child that there was not enough bread in all of Poland to atone for the sins of the Jews in "America, may the Holy One forgive them and may they live to see the error of their ways."[12] Mazel is not without some limits, apparently.

Mazel is that which "drips from above"; it comes "out of nowhere" into our lives and though *mazel* disrupts, its aspiration is to bring forth good things, enjoyable and amusing feelings, even while it shakes up our equanimity. *Mazel* is not subject to necessity; rather, it is the surprising, the incongruous, the fortuitous that *razes* the ordinary and inexorable. When *mazel* comes dancing in, smiles and laughter follow, much as Miriam's skirts swirled as she danced after the Israelites escaped from the tyranny of Pharaoh (Exod 15:20–22).

We also see *mazel* at play when Moses encounters the bush that burns within but is not consumed, and when Mary, a virgin, will bear God's very son within her belly. I think the leper who was healed and turned back to glorify God is similarly a recipient of *mazel* (Luke 17:11–17).

Mazel is the exorable of the inexorable. At work in the universe is a contingency that does not let the immediate and the necessary have full reign. In this drama of necessity and contingency, faith also abides. It is the place where God meets us and invites us to play. Plans are made, actions determined—*mazel* pays us a visit. What now?

Samuel Wells does a marvelous job of showing how to engage the various powers of necessity and contingency. We may not know the future, but we live into that future with the choices we make and our response to the choices of others. Wells proposes the use of improvisational skills that both equip and shape us to make ethical decisions and open alternative stances to those offered. Improvisation frees us from cutting short the options, either silently enduring or fearing where we go with those options. Improvising underscores the necessarily dramatic nature of our lives lived before God and in God's astonishing world.

11. Goldstein, *Mazel*, 99.
12. Goldstein, *Mazel*, 99.

Wells further reminds us that the future is filled with surprises not fears because it is God's story and God has invited us to engage this future: "The vocation of each Christian is to continue to be part of the story, to embody the story from the moment of baptism, regardless of the cost."[13]

With skills of improvisation, contingency becomes a companion as we seek different outcomes than those foisted upon us. Wells provides many examples where humor can function as an instrument to find new options for the intransigence of many political, social, and ethical strategies.

Humor results from *mazel*-moments and can generate *mazel*-moments. Improvisation, a key strategy in much humor, gives us the freedom to imagine various ways and outcomes, rehearse them, and test them with others. Humor may seem like *mere* play or even a trivial response. Wells, however, assures us that taking "time for the trivial is a sign of faith, not foolishness. The church can afford to take the risk of the humorous and ephemeral, because the joke is God's and the laughter is divine."[14] *Mazel*, that imp of metaphysics, is a friend not a foe as we live into

> *The future is not to be feared. Jesus reminded the people of his day with these words: "Look at the birds of the air; they neither sow nor reap nor gather into barns, and yet your heavenly Father feeds them. Are you not of more value than they? And can any of you by worrying add a single cubit to your span of life?" (Matt 6:26–7, KJV). It is not even necessary to know the size of a cubit to grasp Jesus' admonition.*

> *Improvisation is not unfamiliar to God: "Then God's Message came to me: 'Can't I do just as this potter does, people of Israel?' God's Decree! 'Watch this potter. In the same way that this potter works his clay, I work on you, people of Israel. At any moment I may decide to pull up a people or a country by the roots and get rid of them. But if they repent of their wicked lives, I will think twice and start over with them. At another time I might decide to plant a people or country, but if they don't cooperate and won't listen to me, I will think again and give up on the plans I had for them" (Jer 18:5–10, The Message).*

13. Wells, *Improvisation*, 105.

14. Wells, *Improvisation*, 69.

God's future. *Mazel* and improvisation create space for playfulness, joy, and faith to roam.

Humor delights in showing us what we haven't seen in any given situation. Humor is one skill in living out the "none of the above" in our multiple-choice question of actions open to us.

*

For I know that we laughers have a gross cousinship with the Most High, and it is this contrast and perpetual quarrel which feeds a spring of merriment in the soul of a sane man.

—HILLAIRE BELLOC, *THE PATH TO ROME*, 113

It is quite likely that the people of ancient Jerusalem winced at the acerbic wit of the prophet Micah (Superiority). Some likely guffawed with joy at the story of Sarah producing "Isaac/Laughter" at age ninety (Relief). When Jesus said that the Pharisees polish the outside of the cup while leaving the inside filled with dregs, the crowd, no doubt, immediately caught the *inconsistency* of such actions (Incongruity).

These general theories of humor are not mutually exclusive and actually function quite nicely side-by-side. Furthermore, pigeonholing the stories and poems to a particular theory holds little interest to me; naming the particular form of humor does not make it any more funny. Humor is adroit, cagey, ever wary of exposure. Humor *dissembles*—only to make space for good things to run wild.

My interest in the present study is relatively modest: What situations, words, thoughts, and/or occasions in particular texts of Scripture might suggest humor as a rhetorical feature of the text?

Throughout Scripture, play, mirth, humor, and their companions poke the eye of the inevitable and the necessary; they contrive with improvisation to live with expectancy and hope. Exigency is biology; *mazel* is theology. Gaiety bids *mazel* to show her face. We laugh, sometimes with relief, sometimes out of surprise, other times with a knowing smile. Whichever manner we laugh, the invitation of humor is towards playfulness and joy, even as we do justice, love kindness, and walk humbly with God (Mic 6:8).

Mazel-moments step on our toes. Improvisation gives us the tools to navigate these wondrous moments.

It must surely be an egregious display of *hubris* or foolishness to offer a summary paragraph after all the cautions I have noted about humor. However . . . having considered this wild, wonderful world of mirth and humor in Scripture, I offer these three simple sentences (humor doth flourish in threes!):

Humor, if funny, aims to bring about awareness and change, not merely entertain us. It has an implicit invitation to *examine* our assumptions, thoughts, and behaviors. Finally, it is a call to engage in thoughts and actions whose aims are to reconcile, not condemn.

The stories and passages examined in this study are offered as possibilities for humor's presence in Scripture. If any of this rings true, then God has been at the improv long before it was cool.

HUMOR, If Funny

Taxonomies of humor all fail at some point. Having said that:

Humor, *If Funny*, must have an "ouch"—but cannot harm . . . it wounds but must not kill.

Humor always has a point to make; it falls short if it is mere diversion. Pure senselessness and foolishness are not funny; neither is blunt spitefulness.

Humor, *If Funny*, must have a Huh?-Ha! moment—a solvable puzzle . . . it must surprise us, but not bewilder us. It is the Logic of the Absurd, not simply absurd.

Humor questions the obvious that we simply assume and invites us to see the obvious that we're not seeing.

Humor, *If Funny*, must be a tutor—not a philosopher or theologian.

If humor is didactic it will not amuse.

Humor, *If Funny*, must sit on the head of a pin—it cannot fall right or left.

Humor doesn't work if it is too obtuse or too explicit.

Humor, *If Funny*, seeks to woo—not command . . . it may bite but doesn't draw blood.

Humor seeks to amend; it instructs more than demeans.

Humor is protean, allusive and elusive; it hurts and heals. It both challenges the status quo and points us back to time-honored wisdom; it teases and tests. Humor cannot be reduced to a single source or function. It questions both contingency and necessity on a case-by-case basis. It shows obliquely what is overlooked directly. Humor seeks to educate and reform; it is an adjustment opportunity.

Reductionist definitions or approaches to humor always fall short, most especially because humor exposes reductionist appeals of all kinds. Humor is a master magician, a high wire artist, and a supple gymnast. Humor escapes confinement with a wink, frustrates; she is mercurial, capricious. Humor *is gleeful.*

Jokes dissected end up as frogs do when dissected: DOA. Humor itself, however, is the master dissector of the human condition. Humor uses a scalpel, not a hacksaw.

> Some humor seeks to entertain
> Some humor seeks to correct
> Some humor seeks to destroy
> *Sacramental humor seeks to heal.*

But Is It Funny?

> With parables and jokes both, if you've got to have it explained,
> don't bother.
>
> —FREDERICK BUECHNER, *WISHFUL THINKING*, 67

Humor often doesn't translate well from one time to another, or from one situation to another. Sometimes we tell a humorous incident, nobody laughs, and we say, defensively, "Well, you had to be there . . ." Moreover, what one person thinks is hilarious may be only amusing to another, and banal to a third person.

Yet, so far as we can tell, all peoples, societies, and clans engage in humor and laugh. If humor is universal, why it is that so few people find humor in Scripture? R. P. Carroll confidently states, "The concept of a humorous biblical prophet is an oxymoron," and goes on to say, "Humor as we know it today is not a feature of the Bible."[1] Is this truly the case? I suspect that Carroll is cautioning readers of Scripture not to move too quickly and easily from ancient Israel to our contemporary societal norms.

Given that caution, the words and situations, the characters and incidents portrayed in Scripture often point us in certain directions in our reading. Narrative suggests certain types of questions, whereas poetry

---

1. Carroll, "Among the Prophets," 169. I think the operative phrase for Carroll is "as we know it today." I will concede this point: humor as we know it *today* is probably not part of the Bible any more than love (and marriage, etc.) as we know it today is a feature of the Bible. But this is a minor point, maybe even trivial and pedantic. Contemporary British humor and American humor are not "the same" and often do not carry well from one side of the Atlantic to the other, yet, even as an American, I would be hard-pressed to say that the concept of a humorous Brit is an oxymoron. The ancient Hebrews loved and married—and joked—no doubt, in a different idiom than "we" do, but they still engaged in such activities and we can still speak about those activities without being anachronistic or solipsistic. The points of contact are as important as the differences, and both can be taken into account without losing sight of either.

suggests other kinds of questions to ask of a text. Considering humor in biblical texts is one tool among others to employ in reading Scripture.

An obvious question arises: How do we know if something is funny? In one sense humor seems relatively simple and straightforward—you either laugh or not. We all have been in situations where a joke was told and somebody didn't laugh. Perhaps they didn't "get" the joke. Maybe they just didn't think it was funny.

The first thing is to recognize that laughter is *not* the litmus test for humor.[2] Laughter is only one indication of humor—and not an entirely reliable one. We have to rely on clues beyond laughter. There are at least four scenarios that may be true with any given humorous incident.

> We get it—and laugh
> We don't get it—and don't laugh
> We get it and don't laugh
> We don't get it and laugh anyway.

Any of the above can be true for any given humorous incident.

Not laughing at a humorous situation is nearly as common as laughing. Humor can be unfunny, insensitive, or plain hurtful. A person can be amused, stymied, or downright uncomfortable. Jack Handy, from *Saturday Night Live* famed for his "deep thoughts" said, "Whenever I see an old lady slip and fall on a wet sidewalk, my first instinct is to laugh. But then I

There is the famous philosophical conundrum that asks, "If a tree falls in the woods and nobody is around to hear it, does it make a sound?" The answer lies in the definitions of terms. Sound is technically the motion of air, a vibration, so if there is nobody around, nobody would hear it. George Berkeley (d. 1753), British Empiricist Philosopher, argued that case. My question is this: If somebody slips on a banana peel and nobody is around to witness it, is it funny? My answer is a resounding "yes." A colleague and friend of mine was coming out of the Student Union Building at a small college campus over winter break when he slipped on an icy step and landed on his bottom. Nobody was on campus—except me, warmly ensconced in my office opposite the entrance to the Student Union grading papers. I feel personally responsible for his fall because if I were not there, then nobody would be around to witness it, and he would not have fallen. Over thirty years later he still holds me responsible—and I still laugh!

2. Mary Douglas makes this observation in "Joke Perception," 361–76.

think, what if I were an ant and she fell on me, then it wouldn't be quite so funny."

Jack Handy is either horribly insensitive, cruel, . . . or simply funny since, for some strange reason, slipping on something—even something as innocuous as a banana peel—is stock humor.

*

Jokes are always arguments . . . [Teaching] . . .
is a matter of telling jokes . . .

—NICHOLAS LASH, "MINISTRY OF THE WORD
OR COMEDY AND PHILOLOGY," 476–77

At least three skills are needed for humor to work: expertise in crafting or designing the joke or comic element; dexterity in delivering the joke; and proficiency in receiving the joke. These skills are interwoven, but—contra Buechner—these skills can be learned. In fact, most of us unconsciously learned the basics of these skills when we first learned to play "peek-a-boo," and, later tell the more sophisticated "knock-knock" jokes. That doesn't turn us all into great stand-up comedians, but it does indicate the possibility to develop skills in recognizing and enjoying humor in a different culture, even the Ancient Near Eastern culture of the Bible.

To start to develop those skills, I offer the following example.

"A priest, a prophet, and a prostitute walk into a bar . . ."

The form is fairly recognizable, at least in our contemporary Western cultures. Often this form would be signaled by an overt directive, "Have you heard the one about . . . ?" I would argue, though, that the series, usually a threefold series, the repetition of the letter "p" in all three words, and the fact that they have particular social roles begs a question: "What do these three persons have in common?" The *form* draws us into a story; it is a rather odd trinity. It is a puzzle, a conundrum to ponder, consciously or not.

This conundrum is furthered, I suspect, by the different behavioral expectations we have of each member. Humor arises out of specific cultural and social conditions. Priests and prophets aren't always the best of friends but, on the surface, they have more in common with each other than with the prostitute.

Perhaps the biggest conundrum is a likelihood factor. What are a priest and a prophet doing in a bar? It's not illegal, but that is not the usual place to find a priest or a prophet. I'm more likely to accept a prostitute being in a bar—but I suspect there is a degree of chauvinism on display in that assumption. What is least likely is that all three would be in the same bar, at the same time. For the joke to work I have to suspend certain assumptions and accept that the three are in a bar at the same time.

The likelihood factor is one of the trickiest aspects of humor. The joke is thwarted if someone says, "That is absurd that a prophet, a priest, and a prostitute would be in a bar together." Hence, one must accept a special form of absurdity, what Nash calls the "logic of the absurd," for a joke to work.[3] The audience must accept the "joke-world" as presented by the teller, that this particular incident could actually happen, even though it's questionable under normal conditions. Simply being absurd will not ensure laughter. A degree of credibility within the joke-world itself or a trust in the bearer of the humorous incident is necessary.

For humor to work, we must accept that these three persons could be in a bar together.

Something must happen at this point. There must be some exchange between the characters that lends credibility that they would be in a bar together. The something that happens has to be surprisingly believable, at least in a local sense. If we find out that they are siblings, then there is no real conundrum and we move on, without laughing. The something that happens must be *surprisingly apt* and tie the three together in some way that was not obvious on the surface level. Indeed, "surprise" is the operative word and "apt" holds the humor together. If we learn that the priest and the prophet are from the planet Pluto—assuming it is still considered a planet!—then we are surprised, but it doesn't really tie them to the prostitute. It isn't absurd so much as simply strange and unlikely.

There is, thus, a precarious balancing act in humor. Just ask any would-be comedian or comedy writer.

To keep something balanced requires a lynchpin.[4] In humor this pin is the locus upon which the joke-world turns. The story told by the humorist must make an abrupt shift within the elements in the joke-world, a

---

3. Nash, *Humour*, 103–23.

4. Nash describes this as a "trigger," a word or action that dances most often on the point of some dual principle; an ambiguity, an "overt appearance and a covert reality"; Nash, *Humour*, 7.

duplicity on the part of the author (or a character within the story), and yet maintain an overall unity in the piece.

To state this notion of duplicity more technically, humor generally has two "scripts" going on, one more obvious than the other. These scripts converge at a point and one realizes, "Oh, not X but Y!" The shift from one script to the other causes some disequilibrium; we move from a "huh" moment to a "ha-ha" moment. The imbalance is only momentary, but necessary. If the movement from one to the other is obvious, it's not funny; it is also not funny if the movement remains obtuse.

Humor works largely on ambiguities and surprises, which means there is no certainty that a word or incident will be received as intended, and it means that a humorous intent is just as likely to be missed as received. However, it also means that the presence of ambiguity and linguistic or social oddities in a situation opens a discussion of whether humor is present or not. (This point is particularly important in ancient texts or from social contexts where we have little familiarity.)

Cadences and word choices also signal humor. In our joke above we have a series and a recurring "p" sound that draws affinities between the characters that may not be noticed otherwise. If we replaced "prostitute" with another word to characterize the third person, the nature of the joke is changed considerably, and likely would not be funny at all.[5]

Thus language, social, and cultural factors all conspire to play with us as an audience. Humor doesn't conform to norms and propriety, be they lexical, grammatical, or social. Expectations are thwarted. Humor is deft and requires a degree of apprehending on the part of the audience. We must also remember that humor reserves the Cheshire cat smile and the ability to disappear before our eyes.

In the end we learn humor by "trial and error." Mostly error.

*

> And two men who agree about the (lexical) "meaning" of *comic*
> would not necessarily find the same things funny.
>
> —C. S. LEWIS, *STUDIES IN WORDS*, 103

I was in a group setting once when an otherwise dignified and gracious lady commented on an uncomfortable exchange between two people.

---

5. For example, if we used "seductress" or something crass or colloquial, the scenario isn't humorous at all. It's simply odd or vulgar.

After the incident she said, "Well, that was a bit of a *kerfuffle*, wasn't it?" The combination of this gracious lady making a measured judgment on a heated exchange, and then using the unusual word "kerfuffle" was both charming and hilarious. "Kerfuffle" is humorous in and of itself (some words are just like that, fun to say). We have even developed a whole vocabulary to name such odd words and tactics in communication. "Kerfuffle" is categorized as "onomatopoeia,"[6] words that sound like what they do. "Honk" is another such word. Someone who blows his nose and honks when he does it is always good for a laugh. (We dearly try to hide our bodily functions and noises!)

This observation about the sounds and meanings of words bring to the forefront the importance of "delivery" and "reception" as roles in humor. If my friend had said "commotion" it probably wouldn't have been funny at all, although "brouhaha" might have worked or "fracas." Still, say "kerfuffle" and try not to smile . . . it tickles the tongue.

For something to actually be funny also requires a degree of skill in delivery. What is worse than a joke told wrong? We have directives in our culture for signaling a joke: "Have you heard the one about . . . ?" We also have visual clues, like a wry smile or a wink to signal humor. We're obviously not likely to find or even recognize such directives, should they exist in ancient texts. (Did Chaucer ever say, "Have you heard the one about . . . ?")

Recognizing humor in ancient texts is not easy, but it is possible if we pay attention especially to the sounds and meanings, and what context an author presents them. Authors "paint" pictures with words. Consider Jonah being "spewed out" of the whale. Say what you will, you have to be either totally disgusted by the image or break out in laughter.

Unimaginative people are seldom humorous.

*

> Nobody can appreciate the crackers of humour unless he is content to put on his fool's cap with the rest of the party.
> —RONALD KNOX, *ESSAYS IN SATIRE*, 32

Appreciating a joke requires skill in recognizing and receiving the humor, and a willingness to do so. It includes understanding the awareness

---

6. Personally, I think "onomatopoeia" is funny in and of itself. The best way to pronounce it is *fast*—and keep on with the sentence as if you know that you pronounced it correctly. It's a strategy that the character Lucy often used in the *Peanuts* cartoons, especially when she was the "psychiatrist." (Act like you know what you're talking about and most people will think that you do, even if you don't.)

of significant events, social issues, cultural contexts, various roles and ste-reotypes, shared history, and appreciation of certain comedic tropes that may cross times and boundaries (for example, slapstick, sarcasm, pratfalls). In ancient texts like the Bible, having a degree of fluency in the language is helpful to alert a person to the nuances and echoes of words, and maybe even some social roles.

If these skills of structure, delivery, and reception come together, and humor is shared, then we not only laugh, but experience some intimacy. Cohen says that in sharing a joke or humorous incident you "want to reach me, and therein verify that you understand me, at least a little, which is to exhibit that we are, at least a little, alike. This is the establishment of a felt intimacy between us."[7]

> *My friends tell me that I have an intimacy problem. But they don't really know me.*
> *—Garry Shandling, comedian*

We obviously don't have access to most of these clues in an ancient text as opposed to a living culture. Looking for humor in Scripture is complicated because basic knowledge of events, cultural issues, even linguistic skills can make potentially comic incidents largely opaque to us.

But we can learn to recognize some *structural* clues that open the possibility, if not the likelihood, for humor to exist in Scripture. Noticing such things as directives, wordplays, series and sequences, exaggerations or minimizations, surprising turns, ambiguities and incongruities, and the like can alert us to the possibility of humor. We're not likely to recognize the skill of delivery, but certain responses of the original audience might also signal a comedic moment.

There is one final factor: ultimately we also must be willing to put on our "fool's cap" and join the party. We must be willing to go beyond analysis and enter into the text, follow the biblical writers on their terms, ready to laugh along with them.

By way of example, let us turn to a passage that has long been viewed as humorous, one I term "Maybe Not as Funny as You Think."

7. Cohen, *Serious Larks*, 29.

> He laughed the way geese gaggle, less from mirth
> than brainless barnyard rote.
>
> —FREDERICK BUECHNER, *GODRIC*, 69

There is a passage in Amos that smacks of being very sarcastic and wildly funny. It is an indictment of the wealthy and powerful women in the Northern Kingdom in the eighth century BCE. Amos 4:1–2 reads:

> Hear this word, you cows of Bashan
> who are on Mount Samaria,
> who oppress the poor, who crush the needy,
> who say to their husbands, "Bring something to drink!"
>
> The Lord God has sworn by his holiness:
> The time is surely coming upon you,
> when they shall take you away with hooks,
> even the last of you with fishhooks.

Martin Luther says of this passage, "He is addressing those wicked women of the impious. He calls them 'fat cows.' After all, this sex is much too weak to be able to use prosperous situations which even otherwise generally weary the minds of even the wise." He goes on to get a dig in at those in his own day, "the wives of bishops, priest, and princes, to whom the goods of the poor are prey."[8]

When commenting directly on the "fat cows" image, Luther says, "This class by nature has a tendency to be given over to such things unless fear is added."[9]

Ellen Davis cautions about how we read this "bovine metaphor": Yes, these words are to "shock and offend" us but not so much as a sexist comment, as we might read it (and as Luther does little to assuage!).[10]

What is sometimes missed are the geographical images in the passage, Bashan and Mount Samaria. Bashan is the name for the large agricultural district east of the Sea of Galilee. Amos, however, couples Bashan with Mount Samaria, the royal citadel further to the southwest. Amos does a

---

8. Luther, *Minor Prophets*, 150.

9. Luther, *Minor Prophets*, 150.

10. Davis, *Opening*, 229.

bit of "bait and switch" (or "guilt by association"?) here with the locales. In doing so, Amos brings to the forefront the aristocracy, composed largely of absentee landowners. Davis observes that by conjoining these two locales, the focus shifts to the *economy* of the "royal cronies" more than "women's bodies." A translation that highlights the corpulence of the wives misses the more important "economically freighted" metaphor.[11]

It still is a stinging comment, but not a gender freighted one. Davis concludes, "An audience of Israelite farmers might recognize what is implicit in the metaphor: domesticated cows are 'loyal' to anyone who feeds them."[12] Maybe the image gibes powerful men being milksops more than pampered wives being demanding.

In the end, the question is less whether there is humor in Scripture, and more whether we have the skills and patience to tease it out.

11. Davis, *Opening*, 229.
12. Davis, *Opening*, 229.

The Laughters of Faith

He kept quiet: lacking imagination as he did, when a word began to
have one meaning, he couldn't conceive of its having any other.

—ITALO CALVINO, *COSMICOMICS*, 87

In the beginning was not a bang but a chuckle. To say that, however, is
to get ahead of the story. Not all stories start at the beginning; chronological narration is only one way to tell a story. Stories are usually circuitous and may include false promises and hidden obstacles. Events often unfold more like a slinky than a carpet.

. We start instead with a movie, *A Man for All Seasons*, about the great statesman and theologian Sir Thomas More. In one striking scene King Henry VIII jumps off a boat and lands ankle-deep in the mud. Nobody laughs . . . until the king laughs.

This scene from *A Man For All Seasons* and our responses prompt questions about the nature of laughter and humor. It is virtually impossible not to laugh when anybody slips on the

There is a classic scene in the Woody Allen futuristic movie, Sleeper, *where his character, dressed in a tuxedo, flees from authorities. He comes across a garden that has giant fruit and vegetables. He peels a ten-foot banana, ostensibly to hide in, but the authorities catch up to him. While attempting to escape, Woody Allen slips on this giant banana peel. In turn the cops similarly slip on the banana peel. Woody Allen then grabs a huge strawberry, bops a cop over the head with it, and says, "My God, I've beat a man insensible with a strawberry!" To this day, if anybody slips on anything—and is not hurt!—I recall that scene and laugh, saying, "Sorry, I just couldn't help myself." I also keep an eye for any person eating strawberries.*

proverbial banana peel and is not seriously hurt. Do we laugh simply as a response to external stimuli, such as tickling or a pratfall? Such laughter comes as a *relief* of sorts. Nobody got hurt.

However, is laughter more than a stimulus-response action? Do we not also laugh because in certain social contexts, laughter is the expected behavior? When our boss tells a joke, funny or not, we laugh. King Henry's subjects only laughed after Henry laughed. Laughing with the laughter of others shows that laughter is infectious. If this is true, then is laughter a *social* interaction?

Still, why does Henry laugh? After all, he is dressed in nice clothes and lands knee-deep in mud. If that is not bad enough, he does so in front of everyone. Normally Henry does not wear humiliation well. This manner of slipping, however, is especially funny if somebody is well dressed, pompous, or is an authority figure. King Henry is all three.

Henry—and his subjects—laugh at the *incongruity* of the noble king landing unceremoniously in the mud.

The most fundamental question of the universe may well be: Why laugh at all?

*

> I found the whole modern world talking scientific fatalism; saying
> that everything is as it must always have been, being unfolded
> without fault from the beginning. The leaf on the tree is green
> because it could never have been anything else. Now, the fairy-tale
> philosopher is glad that the leaf is green precisely because *it might
> have been scarlet.*
>
> —G. K. CHESTERTON, *COLLECTED WORKS*, 1:262
> (EMPHASIS ADDED)

The first time anybody is said to laugh in Scripture comes with God's chosen couple, Abraham and Sarah. They both laugh when God tells them they will have a child. I find it charming that God specifies that the child will be born in the spring, the time when cattle foal and flowers bloom. An apt time indeed for a child that is otherwise born out of season.

In the story of Abraham and Sarah, God constantly changes the directions of their lives. These characters display a richness of responses to these contingencies of life, the universe, *and God's good pleasure*. The announcement that the couple will have the long-promised son nearly a century after their own births is a prime example of God's *mazel*. This announcement evokes a variety of laughters. If the church is built upon a pun—"I will build my church upon this 'Peter'" (*Petra/Cephas* means "rock" in both Greek and Aramaic)—then the synagogue is built upon a laugh (*Isaac* means "laughter" in Hebrew). Abraham, Sarah, and Isaac show the surprising nature of lives lived in the presence of the Almighty. The story is told in Genesis 17, 18, and 21.

The story is simple and simply told, which is characteristic of narratives that draw the reader ever downward in the subtleties of language and relationships. Abraham and Sarah are getting along in years. They have experienced the trials of life: setting up a home, not an easy task for the semi-nomads; building up a portfolio, in spite of a greedy nephew and petty potentates; and "begatting" children, with ancient methods of *in vitro* fertilization (by means of the womb of Hagar; Gen 16). These trials are largely behind them, as evidenced by the giving of the covenant in Gen 17. Indeed, God marks the significance of *Abram* and *Sarai* at this point in their lives by giving them names reflective of their status: *Abraham*, the ancestor of a multitude, and *Sarah*, the universal matriarch. The only thing missing is the matriarch's multitude.

Something must be done. God, in typical divine fashion, makes a pronouncement: "Furthermore, I will give *from her* [Sarah, from the previous verse] *to you* a son" (Gen 17:16). The word order makes the promise both clear and emphatic.

Divine decrees demand responses. Abraham first, and then Sarah in the following chapter, respond in a similar and otherwise appropriate manner—they laugh. Why is this response appropriate? Everyday talk—serious discourse—seeks clarity, coherence, and consistency. In everyday communication we seek a singular and stable reality that we can appeal to so that communication can take place; words point to things we see and experience, and we can make ourselves and our requests understood to others. Communication flounders when words mean whatever we want them to.

> "When I use a word," Humpty Dumpty said, in rather a scornful tone, "it means just what I choose it to mean—neither more nor less."
> — Lewis Carroll, Through the Looking Glass, 238

We do, however, experience breakdowns in the communication process. "Put your shoes in the boot while I check the oil under the bonnet" is perfectly understandable—if you have lived in Britain for a time.[1] In normal discourse we will generally filter out any contradictory or inconsistent messages. Failing that, we look for signals that will guide our understanding. We have learned that humorous discourse functions differently from normal discourse. In humor we expect ambiguity, allusion, and other verbal sleights of hand. We expect words to be a bit slippery in jokes. For example: When is a comedian not funny? When he is a half-wit. Comedians are said to be "witty," but a not-quite-so funny comedian would not want to be called a "half-wit."

When God says that Sarah will bring a child to term, Abraham and Sarah are left with precious few options, laughter being perhaps the easiest to swallow. Why? They both are put in an uncomfortable situation. Either God must be crazy, not knowing the reality of his words (God is a half-wit?), or God is being "playful," using words in a slippery fashion (God is being funny). The divine decree seems clear enough. There is no signal to indicate humor, no wink or smile. Is God *sporting* with them?

> *"Much sophisticated humor trades on the distinction between what is said, what is linguistically implied and what is conversationally implied."*
> —Mark Martinich,
> "Theory," 28

In the face of this communication breakdown, Abraham falls on his face (often an act of reverence), but then he laughs. The text says he laughs *in his heart*, usually a sign of disrespect. Sarah also, upon hearing the pronouncement later by the angel, laughs *within* herself. Is there a difference in their laughter?

*

[In the comic insight] we gain an inkling, as it were, of the hang of
things, sometimes even a hint of cosmic beneficence.

—MARIE COLLINS SWABEY, *COMIC LAUGHTER*, V

Divine decrees demand responses. Abraham is in the presence of God, the creator of life itself. Why laugh in the face of this divine decree?

1. The "boot" is the trunk of a car and the "bonnet" is the hood.

The responses of both Abraham and Sarah imply some question as to the meaning of God's word to them.

Is Abraham *tickled pink* by God's remarks? In this case, Abraham is momentarily caught off guard by God's words: "Sarah?"—obviously not since her biological clock tocked long ago. "Ah! Ishmael, of course"—derivatively, naturally, but no less Sarah's in that cultural context. Serious discourse, normal communication, has failed, and Abraham sees the obvious failure: Barren women don't bear sons. Does Abraham make a quick interpretive move to *disambiguate*—clarify—the incongruity between God's promise, and the cause and effect reality of barrenness?

Abraham makes the best sense that he can of God's remarks. God can't mean Sarah, obviously, so God must mean someone under Sarah's matriarchal claim. If not, God's statement seems more cruel than funny. At best it is a *faux-pas* on God's part.

Perhaps Abraham's laugh is a face-saving strategy. Abraham's laughter signals a social interaction: "Taking you [God] literally would be absurd so I'll assume that you are being playful, and we can laugh this all off."

Some of the rabbis chide Abraham for his lack of faith. When someone does something in his/her heart, it is usually wickedness or disrespect: "Now Esau hated Jacob because of the blessing . . . and said *in his heart . . .*" (Gen 27:41). However, righteous reflection is often signaled by speaking to one's heart as well: "Now when the Lord smelled the pleasing odor, he said *to his heart . . .*" (Gen 8:21). We are left to ponder the cause and nature of Abraham's laughter.

Among commentators, Abraham is nearly everyone's darling. Calvin is eminently quotable here: "Hence we also infer that he laughs, not because he either despised, or regarded as fabulous, or rejected, the promise of God; but, as is common wont to happen in such things which we least expected, partly exulting with joy, and partly being carried beyond himself in admiration, he breaks forth into laughter."[2]

Calvin is saying that Abraham laughs out of amazement, joy, even admiration. Abraham's is the laughter of belief, not unbelief in this reading. What of Sarah's laughter? In normal discourse, we signal humor and other non-unitary communication with some prefatory gesture or remark. If not, we risk being misunderstood or, maybe, being deceptive. If we are lying, we don't look someone straight in the eye; if we are joking, we smile, roll our eyes or otherwise signal that we're not to be taken seriously. Sarah

2. Calvin, *Genesis*, 473–76.

was following the Lord's lead here; God looked Abraham and Sarah in the eye and did not smile. The discourse was quite serious in her eyes.

In commenting on Sarah's laughter, Ramban, a medieval Jewish commentator, notes, "Laughter of joy is expressed through the mouth" (as opposed to "within oneself").[3] Gen 18:10–12 reads, "Then one [Angel] said, 'I will surely return to you in due season, and your wife Sarah shall have a son.' And Sarah was listening at the tent entrance behind him. Now Abraham and Sarah were old, advanced in age; it had ceased to be with Sarah after the manner of women. So Sarah *laughed to herself*, saying, 'After I have grown old, and my husband is old, shall I have pleasure?'"

Is Sarah's laughter derisive? Incredulous? Sarah's reply is rather earthy and risqué. The NRSV may be a bit prudish here; the words can be read, "shall a withered garment become moist?" (The final term, *'edenah*, is used only here and can be interpreted as "sexual enjoyment/abundant moisture." The term is appropriately opposite to "withered," so Sarna.)[4]

God calls attention to Sarah's laughter. Instead of denying her laughter, maybe Sarah should have said, "I just couldn't help myself." Or, "Sorry, I was only kidding." Or, better still, "Can't you take a joke?" These responses are generally accepted socially.

Sarah may not laugh with joy, but she deals with the pronouncement honestly. Indeed, she takes God's statement quite literally and seriously—and recognizes that it is seriously ridiculous for ninety-year-old barren women to bear children.

Calvin makes the important observation that Sarah fixed her mind "too much on the accustomed order of nature" and did not give glory to God "by expecting from him a miracle which she was unable to *conceive* in her mind."[5]

Various explanations for Sarah's laughter are offered by scholars. Did she not believe God? Did Sarah think the angels were but mere prophets, and not really messengers from God? One scholar suggests—with early twentieth-century political incorrectness—that Sarah was listening at the door with "true feminine curiosity."[6] Even Calvin questions Sarah's laughter: Sarah was not "transported with admiration and joy" as Abraham was.[7]

3. Ramban, *Genesis*, Gen 8:15.

4. Sarna, *Genesis*, 130.

5. Calvin, *Genesis*, 474.

6. Skinner, *Genesis*, 301.

7. Calvin, *Genesis*, 474.

One must surely wonder what joy Calvin would find at age ninety giving birth to a son.

The predominant view is that Abraham laughs by faith and Sarah by lack of faith. The great German scholar Gerhard von Rad is quite right when he says that the laughter of Sarah contains "no 'religious' idea, but precisely in its *sober realism* it shows how completely incomprehensible this act of God was for all human intellect,"[8] and that Abraham's laughter is "an almost *horrible* laugh, deadly earnest, not in fun . . ."[9] (emphasis added).

The border between belief and disbelief is scarcely discernible in either laugh. It is the *reasonableness* of the promise that is beyond belief.

These responses by readers of the story to Abraham's and Sarah's laughter beg some explanation.

*

Everyone laughs in the future tense, for laughter reverberates with hope: It announces that the world is all right after all, and that it will continue, in its wobbly, quirky, unpredictable way.

—BARRY SANDERS, *SUDDEN GLORY*, 32

Truth be told both Abraham and Sarah "get it wrong."

God is serious. God's discourse and manner signals a serious social interaction; however, the content subverts the reality that we would accept as serious. Sarah will give birth, with or without "pleasure" (that doesn't seem to be a serious issue here). The divine decree presents Abraham and Sarah with disparate realities: a serious form of discourse with an apparently illogical content. Barren ninety-year-old women do not give birth in the unitary—"orderly"—world of biological consequences, let alone logical ones. It is indeed the *sober realism* that is so disquieting. In the face of this sober realism laughter may be entirely appropriate.

The Lord inverts the workings of their consistent, unambiguous, and non-paradoxical world. Neither Abraham nor Sarah can imagine that Sarah would bear a son. Granted Abraham makes an attempt—but no less failed!—by offering Ishmael to God (Gen 17:18). Granted Sarah makes an attempt to laugh off this decree with a ribald joke. In this inversion of

8. von Rad, *Genesis*, 231–33.

9. von Rad, *Genesis*, 230.

biological reality God is acting *comically* by reversing Calvin's "accustomed order of nature" that Sarah, rightly, has so much difficulty conceiving. The Lord is not playing by the logical, social, and biological rules that are so familiar to Sarah and Abraham. Into that reality, God invites them to expand their assumptions: No, not Ishmael, Abraham; and yes, Sarah, maybe a dry garment will become moist again.

The divine decree comes to fruition three chapters later in Gen 21 when the Lord visits Sarah and she conceives. The repetitions of the name/word "laughter" are noticeable, maybe even excessive. Abraham names their son *Yitzhak*/laughter. Abraham circumcises *Yitzhak*/Laughter. We are told Abraham is one hundred years old when *Yitzhak*/Laughter is born. Sarah then says that the Lord has made *tzhok*/laughter for her and that all who hear of this will *yitzhak*/laugh with/at her. The laughter has become infectious. Giggles will out.

Some laugh *with* Sarah, sharing her hard-won joy. Others may laugh *at* her for, as von Rad notes, "talk will now take place among the neighbors."[10] Tongues wag at Sarah for either her barrenness or her brazenness.

The scene concludes with what may be another little quip by Sarah, "Who would have said unto Abraham, that Sarah should have given children suck?" (Gen 21:7, KJV). This "withered garment" has indeed become "moist" even to the point of suckling a child. Yet another *mazel*-moment.

The issue at stake in all this laughing comes in Gen 18:14, when God says, "Is anything too wonderful/difficult for the Lord?"[11] This issue is the underlying reality of *imagining* alternative "worlds" to the one faced by Abraham and Sarah. The world of inevitabilities by which most of us, most of the time, live our lives—the orderly world of cause and effect, of communication that does not break down—is not the fullness of reality in God's eyes.

Mark McCleod argues that we can "make God dance" in our "theorizing" about the world: "Our goal as human theorizers, then, is to make interesting worlds that give God pleasure. And when God takes pleasure, we can feel his pleasure."[12] McCloud's theorizing is akin to both Wells's

---

10. von Rad, *Genesis*, 231.

11. Sarah's joy comes down through various stories. The same language will be used with Mary (Luke 1:37); we also find it with the return to the promised land of the exiles (Zech 8:6). The thought is present as well in the story of Samuel's birth (1 Sam 1:7–18).

12. McCleod, "Making God Dance," 292.

improvisation and Goldstein's *mazel*. This theorizing is accepting God's surprises and living into them most fully.

In effect, God is inviting Abraham and Sarah to *improvise* at this *mazel*-moment of their lives: imagine *this* truth, if you will. In this story of our foundational parents of faith, God takes the lead in inviting them to improvise. God affirms the laughter of Abraham and Sarah, even expanding it to the point of delight with this child, *Yitzhak*/Laughter.

Simply put, in the face of the inevitability and propriety of laws in nature and in society, the Bible displays stories and actions that suggest it all *could be otherwise*.

Mulkay's remarks in another context are tailor-made for what Sarah experiences: "The onerous duty of maintaining a unitary worldview has been replaced by the joyous creation of multiple realities."[13]

> Frederick Buechner says, "All his life long, wherever Jesus looked he saw the world not in terms simply of its brokenness—a patchwork of light and dark calling forth in us now our light, now our dark—but in terms of the ultimate mystery of God's presence buried in it like a treasure buried in a field" ("Journey to Wholeness," 454).

Humor is possible at all because God creates and acts in non-predictive ways. God is always willing and able to *surprise* us. Humor in a text is one of the devices that biblical authors have at their disposal to show that we experience disparate realities, when words and actions sometimes cross rather than remain sequential or parallel. Inconceivable thoughts can turn out to be pleasantly true. Our lives before God are diverse and complex, and the choices and responses are equal to the richness of the experiences that make up our lives. Screech simply says, "The Bible vouches for the laughter but does not explain it."[14] *Mazel tov*, God says.

13. Mulkay, *Humor*, 215.

14. Screech, *Laughter*, 56.

SSSHUSH

Sex and Scatology

(Vignette)

A man of breeding does not punctuate his conversation by . . .
taking his conversation out of the drawing-room! Notwithstanding
the advertisements in the most dignified magazines, a discussion
of underwear and toilet articles and their merit or their use, is
unpleasant in polite conversation.

—EMILY POST, TWENTIETH-CENTURY ETIQUETTE EXPERT

There are certain things that you just don't talk about in public. Sex and
scatology are not socially acceptable subjects in mixed company. After
all, Sarah made her remarks "to herself," not out loud.

There seem to be few discussions of underwear in Scripture, but no
obvious discussions of toilet articles.[1] There are in Scripture, however,
one-liners, sexual jokes, and scatological quips, all subjects polite company
seeks to ignore.

Our Hebrew ancestors were neither prudes nor squeamish. As we
noted in the "Laughters of Faith" chapter, a ninety-year-old woman can
enjoy sex (and have babies!), and hemorrhoids on idol-worshiping enemies

---

1. Ullendorf, "Bawdy Bible," mentions the possibility of undergarments for women in
Isa 3:18–26, and in Exod 28:42 a mention of "linen drawers" for the priests are specified.
Translation of these items are difficult, but the context suggests something of private
garments, 429–30.

seem to be a great practical joke by God (see the "Gods Who Can't God" chapter). Unmentionables are often humorous.

*

Physical faeces are accompanied by intellectual ones.

—M. A. SCREECH, *LAUGHTER AT THE FOOT OF THE CROSS*, 147

Baruch Halpern argues that the assassination of Eglon is the "first locked-room murder mystery."[2] This murder includes a sinister[3] deal, a voiding of the bowels, and an escape out the back door. The story is told in Judges 3:12–30.

Because the children of Israel kept doing "what was evil in the eyes of the Lord," the Lord delivered them into the hands of the Moabites. After nearly two decades of this rule, the children of Israel cried out to the Lord, who then raised up Ehud, "the Benjaminite, a left-handed man" (Judg 3:15).

The Moabite king, Eglon, is described, not by his military prowess but by his portliness. His physique might call to mind words spoken years later by the prophet Jeremiah: "fat as the heifer at grass, and bellow as bulls" (Jer 50:11, KJV).

The Israelites prayed and the Lord raised up Ehud.

Ehud comes to Eglon with a tribute and gets a private meeting, just two leaders, alone in an upper chamber, talking over their disputes. Unbeknownst to Eglon, Ehud has hidden a small, sharp sword ("two mouths" in length) strapped to his *right* thigh, hence hidden from the search that might be done to the usual right-handed soldier.

Once alone Ehud takes the sword from his right thigh and thrusts it into Eglon's belly: "Even the grip entered after the flashing blade, so that the fat closed up behind the blade, for he did not draw the sword from

2. Halpern, "Eglon," 33–44.

3. "Sinister" is of Latin origin meaning "left-(side)"; it was also used to connote threatening or evil intent. Ehud's left-handedness is crucial for his success in deposing King Eglon.

his belly, and feces came out."[4] Ehud then escapes out the back, unnoticed (Judg 3:23).[5]

Eglon's servants eventually come to check on the king. When they see that the doors to the upper chamber were bolted, they surmise that the king was "covering his feet," a euphemism for using the toilet.[6] Halpern suggests that both the locked door and the "stench" tip off the servants that the king was still busy in the privy.

The hero, Ehud, by using his God-given left-handedness and wits escapes unharmed and unnoticed. Halpern calls this story of Ehud and Eglon a "rollicking adventure tale."[7] Fox observes that this story is the "ultimate crowd-pleaser" where the enemy is "ridiculed in scatological terms and dies an incredibly violent death."[8]

The story ends with Ehud returning to the Israelites and leading them to take back control of that region; "So Moab was subdued that day under the hand of Israel. And the land had rest eighty years" (Judg 3:30).[9]

*

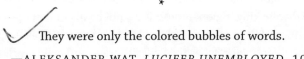 They were only the colored bubbles of words.

—ALEKSANDER WAT, *LUCIFER UNEMPLOYED*, 106

Some quips on characters or incidents come by the later readers of Scripture that seek to explain an obscure incident or phrase. For example, in Gen 12 Abraham and Sarah have gone into Egypt; Pharaoh is struck by Sarah's beauty and invites her into his house (Abraham had failed to

---

4. Fox, *Early Prophets*, 155. Halpern is less delicate: "and the king's anal sphincter explodes" ("Eglon," 34).

5. Halpern goes into a very detailed and technical explanation of the architecture of the rooms and how Ehud escapes unnoticed; those details need not detain us in this discussion.

6. In one list I counted nearly three hundred different phrases for various aspects of "using the loo." "Covering one's feet" was not on this contemporary list.

7. Halpern, "Eglon," 33.

8. Fox, *Early Prophets*, 150.

9. It is noteworthy that the "land" rested for eighty years. "Land" is the most consistent character in Scripture; the health of the land is usually an indication of the health of the people of God. See, e.g., Davis, *Opening*, 62–71, and more fully in her book *Scripture, Culture, and Agriculture: An Agrarian Reading of the Bible*.

mention that Sarah was his wife!). After Abraham and Sarah leave, the Lord strikes Pharaoh with "great plagues" (Gen 12:17). A Midrash explains the "plagues" as *impotence*.

Ellen Frankel offers an alternative midrash on Sarah's story: "When Pharaoh enters Sarah's chamber, an invisible angel saves her from Pharaoh's ardent advances by rapping him on the head each time he approaches her."[10]

Humorous stories or incidents invite these further quips as they are passed along. The Rabbis certainly did not fear being ribald on occasion, especially when it preserved the virtue of their women and poked fun at the manhood of their adversaries.

The apostle Paul moves beyond being ribald to being downright course when he chastises those who were troubling members of the Galatian church over circumcision and falsely accusing Paul of not being consistent in his message. Paul corrects them in no uncertain terms and then concludes, "Why don't these agitators, obsessive as they are about circumcision, go all the way and castrate themselves!" (Gal 5:12). Gundry comments on the force of the words Paul wishes upon these agitators that they "would even get their penises and testicles 'cut off' (or 'chopped off', as his verb could equally well be translated)."[11] Paul is quite blunt here, but also painfully clever, though his adversaries likely took umbrage to his characterization.

Humor is portrayed as "release" but it also works as a defense against those whose clout is brute force, not deftness, cleverness, and skill.

*

Man consists of two parts, his mind and his body,
only his body has more fun.

—WOODY ALLEN

Humor often reminds us that our bodies are only "ours" in a limited sense that we inhabit them for a time. Our bodies are a mainstay of humor.

Body parts and functions are funny; they betray us at every turn. We hide our body parts with clothes and act discreetly with some of our more private noises. Our bodies also require lots of attention; we get tongue-tied,

---

10. Frankel, *Miriam*, 16.

11. Gundry, *Commentary*, 750.

we leak; we don't see things right in front of us, and mishear things clearly stated. We may run and not get weary, but we can also walk and slip on banana peels.

To suppose that the Bible has no bodily or sexual references or humor is inconceivable. Body parts and functions make plain our embeddedness in creation. Circumventing the "bawdy" in Scripture necessarily has unintended consequences, not the least of which is the sheer amusement we can experience as a particular incident unfolds with an indecorous remark or incident.

Sex and scatology, however, do more than entertain. They often show up in literature to undercut taboos, reverse expectations, and knock a person "off his/her game." They are a handy tool for humorists since we work so hard as humans to disguise many of these more personal activities and foibles.

Body parts and sexual humor can also help deal with sensitive or indelicate subjects. Euphemisms display mores or can give contextual clues for attitudes, behavior, and values. Humor, thus, can serve to challenge mores and cultural values, especially when those values no longer hold sway. Anthony Thiselton says that euphemisms begin as "polite metaphors."[12]

Edward Ullendorf, in his classic study "The Bawdy Bible," offers many examples where sexual innuendos and *indelicate* language pepper Scripture.[13] Indeed, before we get out of the first chapters of Genesis we find that the man and the woman have this intimate connection where the man "clings" to this newly minted woman and they become "one flesh" (Gen 2:24).

By the end of Gen 3 they have become aware of their nakedness; the woman is told, "Your desire shall be for your husband" (Gen 3:16b). Fox is a bit more explicit, "toward your husband will be your lust," a translation that Ullendorf advocated for.[14]

This "lust" by women might also play a part where a couple of terms only occur in an otherwise difficult verse in Isa 3:24. The line "instead of a stomacher a girding of sackcloth" (KJV) might be a "protective garment" for women (a "chastity belt" of sorts?).[15]

---

12. Thiselton, *Hermeneutics*, 366.

13. Ullendorf, "Bawdy," 425–56.

14. Ullendorf quotes the Jewish medieval commentator Rashi's rendering, "a desire for intercourse" ("Bawdy," 428).

15. Such garments are known throughout the Eastern Mediterranean in antiquity; Ullendorf, "Bawdy," 430.

Prov 26:6 is another problematic text. Prov 26 as a whole deals with the tomfoolery of the fool. Prov 26:6 reads, "It is like cutting off one's foot and drinking down violence, to send a message by a fool." McKane notes the possibility that the fool has "his legs cut short and *whose buttocks are bare*." He goes on to say that this last phrase is "improbable."[16] Ullendorf, however, considers this rendering a viable option, yet he still glosses the proverb, "Do not send a confidential message by someone who is so obviously unsuited to carry it."[17] The "buttocks" reference would certainly make the proverb more indelible to hearers. More than one Marine Corps drill instructor has told new recruits to get their "head and ass" wired together.

Euphemisms indirectly address sensitive subjects, especially embarrassing or negative in some sense. They also acknowledge something indelicate, holding it lightly, tactfully, and honestly for what it is. Euphemisms can also serve more pernicious purposes, softening violence or hiding truths.[18]

Our bodies are not overly concerned with being dignified or unpleasant. We can hide or deny all we want, but the body will have the last laugh.

16. McKane, *Proverbs*, 597.

17. Ullendorf, "Bawdy," 426. This gloss seems to tame the proverb even more than McKane's does.

18. The comedian George Carlin had a poignant routine regarding the language used for mental damage to some soldiers in battle. In WWI it was called "shell shock." By Vietnam we were no longer shell-shocked but had PTSD—"post-traumatic stress syndrome." He notes that two words have become four, and all the life is drained out of a powerful image.

The Education of a Dove

The comic characters remind us of those toy weighted figures beloved of children that right themselves after every upset with a resilient upswing suggesting a buoyant affirmation of life.

—MARIE COLLINS SWABEY, *COMIC LAUGHTER*, 136–37

The book of Jonah invites playfulness.[1] Jonah, however, doesn't want to play.

God displays a high degree of playfulness with Jonah throughout the book. In response Jonah displays a steadfast recalcitrance towards God's invitation to play. Jonah blocks God's invitations. Even at the end, with all his success, Jonah's unwillingness to play remains intact. Jonah also displays no joy in being perhaps the most successful prophet in history.

Jonah may not want to play, yet he is anything but idle throughout the book.

With every opposition by Jonah to God's invitations, God counters with a series of practical jokes to keep Jonah in the story. God may not laugh, as some assert, but God has a wicked sense of humor, if Jonah is any indication of God's character. These practical jokes are not meant to demean Jonah, but to draw his attention to the fortuitous nature of a life lived in relation to the Almighty. Every act does not have an opposite and equal response; they are always opposite and *unequal*. It's called "grace."

Jonah and God resemble a "cat and mouse" relationship. Since "Jonah" means "dove," perhaps we should change the image to "cat and bird."

---

1. Peterson, *Unpredictable Plant*, 10.

[It] is characterized by bold fantasy, merciless invective and outrageous satire, unabashedly licentious humour, and a marked freedom
of political criticism." [Said of Aristophanes but works equally well
with the book of Jonah.]

—OLIVER TAPLIN & MAURICE PLATNAUER, "ARISTOPHANES"

Throughout the book that bears his name, Jonah is offered a chance
to be part of a larger story of God's work in the world. Jonah is called to
be a prophet, one chosen by God to deliver an important message from
God. Jonah's responses, unpredictable and begrudging acceptances at best,
precipitate further unpredictable and gracious responses by God. When
God says, "Go to Nineveh, that great city and cry out against it" (Jonah 1:1)
Jonah goes—*away*. Jonah's wayward moves prompt further moves by God.
The bird moves and the cat reacts.

God responds to Jonah's refusal by sending a wind to toss about the
ship he boards on his way *away*. Jonah reciprocates by going overboard.
God then sends a whale to save Jonah; Jonah reacts with syrupy-sweet
prayers. The whale sends Jonah out ("vomited") on the shores of Nineveh.
Jonah relents and preaches, perhaps the shortest evangelizing sermon ever.
Jonah is wildly successful. Yet Jonah is not thrilled by his success, so he goes
off to sulk in the sun. God, mercifully, sends a shade tree. Jonah is grateful,
but then sulks all the more when God sends a worm to eat the plant. At
every turn God enlists the created order to draw Jonah back into the story.
Jonah shows no desire to give in to God's overtures. God is simply not *fair*
in Jonah's eyes.

The trajectory of God's pranks begins with Jonah's call, rises in the
storm, subsides with the sailors who find God's favor, plummets when Jonah is swallowed by the fish, gets projected forward with the vomit, reaches
heights by the hearty repentance of the Ninevites, and dissolves with the
qiqayon, a plant sucked dry by a worm. The book of Jonah ends with a
crescendo statement by God, and Jonah's silence. Jonah ends by sheer ex-
haustion. The effect of all these practical jokes is a lesson in God's audacious
compassion. Jonah is all set for an adjustment opportunity.

> A crucial feature of all these comic characters is that
> they cannot be destroyed by shame.
>
> —DAVID ELLIS, *SHAKESPEARE'S PRACTICAL JOKES*, 174

If repentance is the place where we *willingly* put ourselves in a state to see and receive God's audacious compassion, then Jonah never gets the lesson. Jonah succeeds as no other prophet before or after him in calling a wayward people to repentance. Yet Jonah himself never actually repents. The book ends with Jonah's silence in answer to God's pivotal question about the nature of God's compassion: "And should not I spare Nineveh, that great city, wherein are more than six-score thousand persons that cannot discern between their right hand and their left hand; and also much cattle?" (Jonah 4:11, KJV)

To be sure, Jonah knows the language of repentance; he knows the posture, words, and intonations (Jonah 2). Yet even the fish, who eagerly swallows Jonah, has a difficult time swallowing Jonah's prayer of repentance. When Jonah finishes his prayers, "the Lord spoke to the fish and it vomiteth out Jonah upon the dry land" (Jonah 2:11, KJV).

Perhaps Jonah, like the mother in Goldstein's novel *Mazel*, could not conceive that there is enough "bread" (compassion) to atone for the sins of the people beyond their *shetl*. That God's compassion could reach as far as "[America/Nineveh], may the Holy One forgive them and may they live to see the error of their ways."[2]

Whatever we choose to think of Jonah, it is clear that he is a reluctant prophet and shows no apparent shame. It is also clear that God is reluctant to let go of this prophet. God's practical jokes on Jonah direct him to the desired destination and vocation. Practical jokes are a kind of testing, an adjustment opportunity, whereby the "victim" may choose a number of responses. In the language of improvisation, Jonah consistently blocks God's offerings. Ostensibly the destination is Nineveh, but practically it may be Jonah's own heart that is directed. The bird moves again.

---

2. Goldstein, *Mazel*, 99, where the bracketed word is "America," but would be equally apt for "Nineveh" to Jonah.

*

Laughter first, moral later.

M. A. SCREECH, *LAUGHTER AT THE FOOT OF THE CROSS*, 269

An inordinate amount of energy is spent identifying the details in Jonah. This endeavor is undertaken by those who question Jonah's historicity as much as those who accept the story with all its chimerical elements.

The large fish is conventionally a whale but other proposals include "shark," "snake," and "monster." Many readers scour botanical texts to identify the *qiqayon* (the plant appointed by God to shade Jonah near the end of the book; Jonah 4:6). Despite such endeavors, scholars end up flummoxed, bewildered, and nonplussed. Even the *suph*, the plant that adorns Jonah's head in the fish (Jonah 2:5), entangles readers, though we know what this plant is. The *suph* is a reed plant, found in marshlands, and appears mostly in texts referring to Egypt and its marshes (Exod 2:3, 5). What is a "marsh" plant doing in the middle of the sea, in the belly of a fish, nigh unto Nineveh?

The story simply requires a fish big enough to accommodate a full-grown male residing in its belly, a *big* fish. Similarly, Tarshish is of uncertain location. The one thing that we can be certain of is that Tarshish is nowhere near Nineveh.

Stories like Jonah are not uncovered so much in the details as found "in the tale." Humorous tales generally invite a glance backwards once the end of the story is reached. Ambiguous words and events take on different shades in the light of the ending.

Identifying the fish, questioning the presence of marsh plants, and finding Tarshish are not conundrums to solve, but simply part of the teller's tale. They are to be received as part of the *logic of the tale*. In humor there is a logic factor that must be accepted, not solved. It is the "logic of the absurd."[3]

Humor flourishes on exaggeration. In Jonah most everything is *gedol* ("great; magnified"), literally larger than life. The fish, the storm, the iniquity of the people, the plant, and even repentance are supersized. People of sound mind have always scoffed at this story. The story is ludicrous—a

---

3. See, e.g., Palmer, *Logic of the Absurd*.

fish swallows a person whole. Reason suffers greatly here, but the tale is enriched by these elusive and evocative details.

Walter Nash says, "It may seem undignified to allow the ringmaster-humorist to make fools of us in this way [discarding notions of logic and likelihood]; but really, the assent we give to the absurdities of the joke is no more contemptible than the license we allow to the inventions of a fairy tale."[4] We could easily substitute "parable" for "fairy story" since ancient Hebrew narrative does not make these fine distinctions in literary works. *Mashal* (parable, proverb, song) seems sufficient literary designation for our *exaggerated* tale of this reluctant prophet.

Parables generally function much the same way as humor. They work best with delightful acceptance, not niggling scrutiny. If we ignore the logic of Jonah, the logic of the absurd that is necessary in a humorous tale, then we're likely to get as tangled as Jonah in the fish. Nash observes, "Jokers are in the habit of putting up circus-hoops through which their clients must obligingly leap, to achieve the reward of laughter."[5] It is a charitable author who gives us such a tale where we, like Jonah, can either sink or swim.

To question the taxonomy of the fish, the shrubbery surrounding Jonah's head, and the leaf size of a shade plant is to miss the forest for the *qiqayon*. What seems more likely is that the monster of the sea and the marsh plant in the big fish are employed to terrify any self-respecting, agrarian Israelite farmer. Such a person would know enough not to question the tale but delight in the waggish journey of Jonah—and thank God that they live on *terra firma*, not adrift at sea, literarily.

Jonah is arguably the most playful, humorous book in Scripture (though Esther might object to that!). And Jonah the man is among the most self-conscious characters we find in Scripture—and one of the most lacking in grace. He's the perfect person to be the object of pranks, divine or otherwise.

The unrelenting string of practical jokes requires that the likelihood of this tale be held lightly for the enjoyment of this fish story. These practical jokes also invite improvisational responses to the situations Jonah encounters or creates.

4. Nash, *Humour*, 5.

5. Nash, *Humour*, 5.

Such stories . . . mean to bother you.
—PATRICIA HAMPL, "IN THE BELLY OF THE WHALE," 290

While many readers have opted for a more metaphorical reading of the book, Jonah himself is a literalist at heart. Not that Jonah is concerned with the species of fish or the type of foliage around his neck in the belly of the whale, but he seems to receive the divine call more literally than any other prophet that comes to mind. Jonah's call to be a prophet is perhaps the largest practical joke that God plays on Jonah.

Jonah's call to prophecy comes in a line of similar calls. The call of Moses is a textbook example. Moses, shepherding in the middle of the desert, turns aside when he encounters a burning bush not consumed by the fire within. The type of plant is, again, inconsequential to the story. The fire, however, is a cause for curiosity. Moses turns towards the bush—a turning *towards* God, the usual posture of repentance.

God speaks to Moses out of the bush. God has seen and heard the affliction of the people of God and sends Moses to deliver them. Moses, undeniably not a typical shepherd, tries to reason with God: "Who am I that I should go to Pharaoh . . ." (Exod 3:11). Moses becomes the poster child for questioning a call from God. Ostensibly a prophet questions the call out of humility towards such a task. After assurances from God, the prophet goes.

Jonah is fully aware of this pattern and the outcomes. Jonah knows that even entering into a conversation with this God, as Moses, Jeremiah, and others had done previously, will not end with a *figurative* going, say sending a letter to the king of Nineveh. The call will mean a literal going. God says to Jonah, "Get up and go . . ." (Jonah 1:1). Jonah skips the obligatory hesitation to respond to the call; rather Jonah responds immediately, wordlessly, and literally: Jonah goes—due west, not east to Nineveh.

Perhaps Jonah justified this going away by remembering the Moses story. Moses himself questions whether the powerful Egyptians would acknowledge his authority (Exod 3:13–15). Jonah might have reasoned that since the Ninevites don't know left from right (Jonah 4:11), they would not be any more likely to heed Jonah than the Egyptians were to heed Moses. Jonah does literally what other prophets do more figuratively in their response to God's call. Jonah's customary stance is *from* not *towards*.

In reading Jonah it is clear that the author is familiar with the Scriptures, especially the Psalms (Jonah 2). As Jonah departs from God, would the words of Ps 139 echo in his mind? "Where can I flee from your Spirit? If I ascend to heaven, you are there; if I make my bed in Sheol, you are there . . ." (Ps 139:7b–8). In fleeing from God, Jonah goes to the "depths" of the ship, which is the term used in parallel to *Sheol* in Isa 14:15. As Magonet points out, it is God's *ruach* (spirit-wind) that catches up to Jonah on the sea.[6] This is the same spirit-wind that hovers over the chaotic waters when God calls creation into being (Gen 1:2).

These biblical echoes seem more important than the elusive details of the flora and fauna in the story.

Jonah is often as much a mime as he is a prophet throughout the book; he seldom uses his own voice. Jonah's only recorded oracle (his sermon calling the Ninevites to repentance) amounts to five words in the Hebrew: "Yet forty days—Nineveh devastated." Jonah's longest speech is his prayer in chapter 2, consisting of snippets of various psalms. When Jonah does use his own voice, it is often a sullen voice. When God asks if it *pleases* him to be angry at the gourd's lack of shade, Jonah answers, "I'm angry enough to die" (Jonah 4:9). Similarly, when the sailors ask Jonah what to do about the storm on the sea, he replies, "Cast me into the sea" (Jonah 1:12). Unlike Moses, who is "heavy of tongue" (Exod 4:10), Jonah does not lack eloquence, though he is virtually speechless apart from his Commonplace Book of quotations from passages of Scripture and his ire at God (Jonah 4:1–4).

David Ellis, speaking of the practical jokes in Shakespeare's comedies, says, "Practical jokes may often punish what is foolish, anti-social or deviant in their victims, but there is nothing intrinsic in them which prevents their being played on the intelligent, the innocent, or the worthy."[7] Jonah is too clever by half throughout the book; he is a skillful plagiarist and a churlish conversation partner.

Jonah boards a ship headed west to Tarshish, not east to Nineveh, seemingly blocking God's call. Jonah, the literalist, the plagiarist, seems ripe for another adjustment opportunity. Jonah, the "dove," continues his flight *from* God.

---

6. Magonet, *Form and Meaning*, 83.

7. Ellis, *Shakespeare's Practical Jokes*, 173.

Fortune, *who dearly loves such tricks,* was having *a little sport with them* both, and Fortune may show a Chaucerian roughness when she cracks jokes.

—ROBERTSON DAVIES, *THE CUNNING MAN*, 126
(EMPHASIS ADDED)

On the ship Jonah makes his bed in *Sheol*, metaphorically (Jonah 1:5). Now what?

All the flora and fauna of the world are at God's disposal, as well as meteorological resources to encourage this less-than-enthusiastic prophet. Repentance comes easily for the "salty sailors" (the word translated as "mariner" here is the same root as the word for "salt") on the ship, the king of Nineveh and his great and faithless city, and even for the animals of Nineveh (Jonah 3:8). Jonah, however, is one of God's chosen, stiff-necked people. Being chosen and being obedient are not synonymous in Scripture.

God first enlists the wind and waves to help persuade Jonah to obey. Seasoned sailors are fearful and *pray*. They know when things are beyond their ken. Agrarian Jonah sleeps. The sailors repent; yet try as they might, they are unable to get Jonah to repent. Jonah leaves the sailors with precious few options. Man overboard; literally.

This further tactic to evade God's call to prophesy (sleeping through the storm and going overboard) does not deter God. God appoints a fish, big enough to swallow this mulish man. This scene seems akin to a magic trick. Magic tricks work because the audience always focuses on the wrong detail. It's easy to focus on the gargantuan nature of the fish, whereas the real action is Jonah's prayer from the belly of the fish.

Scholars have noted a certain "inappropriateness" of Jonah's prayer of thanksgiving while still in the belly of the fish. Wishful thinking? Hedging his bets? Simple audacity? Jonah has shown us a degree of audacity already, running away from God. Thankfulness for being saved from the sea seems the least likely motivation since Jonah had already issued a death wish by drowning when God sends the wind to encourage Jonah to accept his call as prophet (Jonah 1:12). Jonah will later utter another death wish when God relents of the evil intended for the people of Nineveh after they repent (Jonah 4:3).

The book of Jonah has been called a parody by some. For example, Jack Miles observes that the author deliberately disregards the poetic canon by placing Jonah's prayer in the midst of this tale.[8] Miles says, "His troubles are not like waves washing over his head. His troubles *are* waves washing over his head."[9]

Jonah knows the psalms as well as he knows the call narratives of other prophets. Jonah's prayer is seemingly a model of piety, liberally echoing other psalms (e.g., Jonah 2:3 with Ps 42:7). Later, in Jonah 4:2 after his success as a prophet, Jonah echoes the opening words of the sailors' prayer in Jonah 1:14. Jonah knows how to pray. This prayer in Jonah 2 is largely prayers lifted from the psalms; they have all the right sounds of prayer, but with a hollow ring.

If being swallowed by a *migdol* fish is a practical joke at the end of Jonah 1, by the end of Jonah 2 God reverses that joke: Jonah is *unswallowed* by the fish. More specifically, this fish vomits Jonah out.

Swallowing Jonah is, no doubt, a spectacular feat, but disgorging him is arresting. The word used here is visceral and therefore more conspicuous. The King James Version does well to use "vomited" rather than something tame, like "spit."[10] Most of us can live with an occasional *rejection* of some sort but to be "vomiteth" or "spewed out" goes beyond the pale. Has God taken this practical joke too far?

We might ask another question first: Is it any accident that the vomiting comes *immediately after* Jonah concludes his prayer? It is tempting to call the spewing "ironic" as an answer to Jonah's prayer (as Wolff and others have done; see below). Yet the spewing is rather appropriate if the prayer is felt to be *sickeningly sweet* by the whale, hence not an odd or inappropriate response, as irony might suggest.[11]

Are we meant to feel compassion for Jonah—or the fish? The fish seemingly can't stomach Jonah any more. Does this sickness stem simply

---

8. Miles, "Parody," 168–81.

9. Miles, "Parody," 174.

10. The 1559 Geneva Bible has "cast out," a seemingly puritanical gloss on this otherwise distasteful term.

11. Hugh Kenner makes the point that "irony" meaning something *odd, unintended, embarrassing*, etc. is a misuse of the term; cf. "Ironies about Irony," in *Mazes*, 252–60. An *eiron* in Greek is a dissembler. It seems best to consider whether the author of Jonah is having a straightforward "go at us" using "spewing" precisely here in our story, not just being odd or unintended.

from Jonah's presence, or from his simplistic prayers?[12] Maybe our *theological correctness* sickens God sometimes.

It could be that Jonah himself is "indigestible."[13] It is also possible that it is the prayer that the fish finds so disgusting. Though many have tried to rescue Jonah, it is difficult not to hear a rote or feigned repentance in his prayer "out of the depths." Jonah has the words, but not the heart, apparently, for these gracious words. Wolff notes that the Hebrew word *qy'* ("vomit") is only used on occasions that "rouse disgust."[14] This disgust is felt by animate entities, like the fish, but relative inanimate entities can feel disgust as well. Half the occurrences of *qy'* are found in Leviticus where the land will vomit out its inhabitants for their disregard of God's statutes and ordinances (e.g., Lev 20:22).

Is the fish following suit with the land in Leviticus? Does the fish feel the same disgust with Jonah that the land feels in response to the defiling acts of the people of God (e.g. Lev 18)?

Jonah's prayer, though theologically sound, seems inappropriate in this context.[15] Wolff's assessment is stronger: "But the reader may detect a bitter humor and mocking note in these undignified dealings with Jonah . . . [vomiting] rouse[s] disgust . . . [it is] a coarse word . . . [the satirist] gives scope for the rude laughter of his readers . . . as if [Jonah] were something intolerably indigestible . . . this irony, with all its exaggeration, is slyly absurd rather than bitter."[16] The fish may think it is rather more bitter than absurd, I suspect.

If the author intended to be *delicate* almost any other word would suffice. By expelling Jonah in this manner, the author highlights the joke aspect of practical jokes where reversals are common: the spewing lands Jonah precisely where God had called him to in the first place. Jonah is back on the road to Nineveh, back in the center of the story.

Jonah chooses flight and the sea over the divine call. God improvises to square the circle. That's what God does. Just ask Moses (cf. Exod 4:10–17).

---

12. Strawn, "Vomiting," 452–59.

13. Wolff, *Jonah*, 139.

14. Wolff, *Jonah*, 139.

15. Magonet, "Jonah," 939.

16. Wolff, *Jonah*, 139

If Jewish humor exposes chaos, it exposes no less an unwillingness
to live with chaos, pitting people's expectation of God against God's
of human beings, with no way of guaranteeing the outcome.

—RUTH WISSE, *NO JOKE*, 115–16

Jonah, the "dove," has yet to find peace with God, even at the end of
this story. Jonah continues to block God's offers. As noted above, being
chosen and being obedient are not synonymous in Scripture. In our day
we might characterize Jonah's behavior as "passive-aggressive." Jonah might
counter by pointing out his *strength of character*.

Jonah, the dove, does not allow himself to be defined by others. Neither the sailors, the whale, the Ninevites, nor even God are given the privilege of defining Jonah, though all are willing to assist him.

Jonah knows the distinction between being chosen and being obedient.
With strength of will and bungling through tight situations, he perseveres
by virtue of resistance over compliance. Even when Jonah does fulfill his
role, successfully calling Nineveh to repent, he does so on his terms, with as
few words as possible (as we noted above), "Yet forty days—Nineveh devastated" (Jonah 3:4). Jonah does not allow the circle to be so easily squared.
The cardinal character trait of Jonah is compliance on his terms.

Few prophets succeed in calling even the "faithful" to repentance.
Jonah is *greatly* successful, even calling the faithless to faith. Still, Jonah
has yet to find peace with God. God, however, has not exhausted his bag
of tricks to draw Jonah back towards God. God does not give up on Jonah.
God pursues Jonah throughout the book; indeed, "God desires not only to
reclaim the Gentiles but also to have Jonah *as an understanding friend*."[17]

God counters once again, sending a plant, a worm, and a sultry east
wind. Alas, "For Jonah, only a night's sleep separates full happiness from
abject misery."[18] Jonah is *good and angry*, enough to utter another death
wish when the shade fades away (Jonah 4:3).

Jonah only works as humor if we assume a degree of friendship between Jonah and God. "*Ven mazel kumt, shtels im a shtul.* 'When mazel

17. Davis, *Prophecy*, 53 (emphasis added).

18. Sasson, *Jonah*, 316.

comes, pull up a chair for it.'"[19] God has saved the least-practical joke for last; it may also be the most conspicuous thing necessary in our lives, and the hardest to see some days. It is called *Grace*.

It's quite likely that Jonah did not know the species of the plant at the end of the book. He seems only to know it as a plant that provides shade. Jonah is immediately happy, indeed, he is *big* happy (*migdol*). When Jonah retreats to the desert, he constructs a "booth" (*succoth*, booths constructed by the Israelites in the desert after God's grand act of grace delivering the people of God from Egypt; cf. Exod 33:22; Lev 23:42). The plant appears, like *manna* in the wilderness.

The marsh plant in Jonah 2 required little explanation; however, the *qiqayon* calls for questioning. It brings the tale to an end, though to say it resolves the story would be a stretch. If anything defines Jonah, however, it is the *qiqayon*. The fish, the marsh plant, and Tarshish are exegetical puzzles that scholars can solve; the *qiqayon* seems more an existential puzzle for readers to ponder. It conveys more than it shows.

We noted above that scholars have long foraged for the *qiqayon*. Identifying the plant ranges from "gourd," "cucumber" plant, and even a "pumpkin" plant (the latter is unlikely since it wasn't grown in that region in antiquity). Jerome's suggestion that it is a "castor oil" plant seems to win the day by most scholars. The castor oil plant is appropriate since it gives shade and is rather obnoxious.[20] Though an obnoxious plant may be fitting for this *errant dove*, visualizing it may not be quite as important as *listening* to it.

All the characters in Jonah merit attention; the *qiqayon* pays dividends when pondered. Because the plant seems more of an existential puzzle than exegetical problem, the *qiqayon* may have an "interpretive bounty."[21] God invites such consideration when God asks Jonah, "You have compassion for the *qiqayon* for which you have done less than nothing . . . should I not have compassion for Nineveh—and all the cows?" (Jonah 4:10–11). God invites Jonah to mull things over. *Mulling* is a fitting endeavor for the spiritual life.[22]

Jonah's own name also merits some attention. Jonah has not lived up to his name so far in the book. A "dove" in Scripture is associated with

---

19. Goldstein, *Mazel*, 292.

20. Handy, *Jonah's World*, 93.

21. Fisch, "*Crusoe*," 230.

22. Fisch, "*Crusoe*," 221.

sacrifices in the temple, as a messenger, and an image of God's Spirit, among other things. Jonah is none of the above. Nobody has been allowed to define Jonah, not even God. The *qiqayon* may have this final privilege in the book. Though it is speechless, the plant names Jonah.

Even if the plant is not readily identifiable, *listening* to it is telling. What is noticeable about this particular flora is the unusual form of the word. It appears to be comprised of two words: *qiqa* + *yon*. "*Yon*" is where we hear our character's name, "Jonah"/*Yonah*. We should also recall *qi'* from the whale incident. This particularly form of *qi'* actually intensifies the word's meaning, *double-vomit*. If *qiqayon* is heard in this way, as a play on Jonah's name, it is a puzzle of sorts. Perhaps the plant is a final practical joke on this counter-prophet.

A question just below the surface of this tale has been: What prompts such resistance from Jonah towards God throughout the book? Jonah's anger here is described as "great." What has God done to deserve such contrariety? Improvisation involves risk and is a form of "testing," a common theme in Scripture from Adam and Eve in the garden to Jesus in the wilderness.

Jonah's complaint against God is that he *knew* God's compassion was great, here not a form of "great (of importance)" as usual throughout the book, but "great (abundant, many)." Jonah admits that he knew God does not easily give up and that God would relent if the people of Nineveh repented: "I knew that thou art a gracious God, and merciful, slow to anger, and of great kindness, and repentest thee of the evil" (Jonah 4:2, KJV). What gets stuck in Jonah's craw seems to be God's compassion. God is simply *too* gracious.

Jonah's words, once again, are not his own, but is a *pastiche* from Exod 4:6 and Jer 18:8. Jonah throws God's own words back at God. When the king of Nineveh is given the opportunity to repent, he says, "Who knows? God may relent and change his mind; he may turn from his fierce anger, so that we do not perish" Jonah 3:9, (a virtual quotation itself of Joel 2:14 where Israel turns back to God on a day of disaster). Jonah knows Scripture; the king, however, knows the proper *stance* in the face of compassion offered. Moberly observes:

> God's mercy remains His to give, and He interacts sovereignly and relationally, but not mechanically . . . but they [the repentant] hope in trust rather than presumption . . . The Ninevite construes divine

mercy rightly in both word and action, while Jonah knows enough only to become upset.[23]

Jonah quotes words from God's own lips—though once again we must wonder if this is simply paying lip service to them, as might be the case in Jonah 2. As Moberly observes (regarding Exod 4:6 and Jer 18:8), human response to the prophetic word *matters* to God: "The one passage articulates the gracious and merciful character of God, and the other articulates how that grace and mercy works out, through a *responsiveness that can act mercifully rather than enact a predicted judgment.*"[24]

The author of Jonah knows full well that this is as clear a statement of God's nature as any in Scripture.[25] It also suggests that God's mercy is something to be pondered, a mystery to live, not a formula to calculate. God's mercy comes in the *drama*, the improvisation of divine action and human response. God gives the final word in Jonah. Readers are left to wonder how Jonah responds to this word, thus becoming participants themselves, maybe even an understanding friend.[26]

*

> [The chief feature of *Comedy*] is that it ends happily,
> usually with a marriage.
>
> —DAVID ELLIS, *SHAKESPEARE'S PRACTICAL JOKES*
> (OFTEN SAID OF SHAKESPEARE'S COMEDIES)

God has shown a high degree of patience with Jonah; Jonah has not reciprocated. The time is now past for practical jokes. It's time for *practical theology*. God queries Jonah: "You have *chus* (compassion) for the *qiqayon*, should I not have *chus* for the thousands of Ninevites who also repented?— and don't forget the cows!" The Ninevites do not have *Torah* to guide them, they don't even know left from right (Jonah 4:11). God's appeal is to "natural theology" not dogmatic theology at this point.[27]

---

23. Moberly, *Theology*, 195.
24. Moberly, *Theology*, 193 (emphasis added).
25. Moberly, *Theology*, 192.
26. See Davis, *Prophecy*, 53.
27. Moberly, *Theology*, 209–10.

Jonah knows the language and posture of *chus*, and even the source of it, just as he knows the prayers of the people of God. However, on his own initiative, Jonah has determined the limit of God's compassion. Harold Fisch, in an essay about the novel *Robinson Crusoe* (itself a reworking of the Jonah story) observes, "[Robinson Crusoe] has to learn what it means to live by the grace of God; that is the nature of the trial in the desert."[28] There is, as Wells notes, a *drama* to our lives in response to God's work in the world, one that requires improvisation based on habits developed and tried in concrete situations, rather than mere repetition or even originality.[29]

Moberly observes that *chus* is a "heart issue" shown primarily through the tear ducts, more than a remembrance of quotes past. Jonah may have benefitted from remembering his fellow prophet Micah's last words on God's actions. Micah says that God will even subdue our iniquities and cast them into the *depths of the sea* (Mic 7:19). This is, of course, where Jonah began his journey towards Nineveh.

The practical jokes work as humor because Jonah proves his intransigence, ignoring God's *chus* even, so it seems, to the end. Jonah, who has been the beneficiary of God's *chus* at every turn, begrudgingly extends that same *chus* to others.

Perhaps it is no accident that the most consistently humorous book in Scripture is also one of the clearest statements of God's mercy and forgiveness.

Swabey observes that in the "so-called nonsense humor [Edward Lear; Lewis Carroll], a certain anaesthesia of the heart is clearly present . . . [that] instead of anything following anything indifferently, there shall be a method in the madness, a consistency in its inconsistency, an intelligible logic that makes comic nonsense distinct from nonsense pure and simple . . . Instead of the logic of measure for measure . . . they hold that absurdities and improbabilities rule the world."[30] Or, maybe more simply, God's grace is not bound by our reason or sense of justice.

Were Jonah to experience some shame in all these ventures, find some humor in all his circumstances, he may encounter grace as well. Jonah, however, never realizes this *educative* role of humor. The question, then, becomes ours to ponder as hearers of this tale.

28. Fisch, "*Crusoe*," 29.

29. Wells, *Improvisation*, 59–70.

30. Swabey, *Comic Laughter*, 24–25.

If you're too fine for the funnies, you're too fine for life. . . . Here
they are, you see. A full week's issue of hilarity and hard-bitten
street philosophy. . . . They're not called stereotypes for nothing;
they embody what a majority of people believe, or accept as self-
evident. They make people feel superior to what he can recognize as
the stupidity or folly of somebody else. . . . While the funnies live,
Aristophanes [read "Jonah"] is never quite dead.

—ROBERTSON DAVIES, *CUNNING MAN*, 110

Jonah is on the move constantly throughout the book. Yet Jonah ends
in a stalemate. At the very least we do not see Jonah's unambiguous acceptance of God's offer. I am reminded of something Chesterton says of
the artist James Whistler, "There was no laughter in his nature; because
there was no thoughtlessness and self-abandonment, no humility."[31] Jonah
is self-conscious to the point that he seems unable to extend his hand to
grasp grace.

Sin and grace are not reciprocal relations to Jonah; repentance and
forgiveness seem polar opposites. The logic of the absurd is the very nature
of God's *arithmetic* though. Maybe the cat actually moves first, then the
bird moves; forgiveness is the offer, and accepting the forgiveness is the
repentance. God's prior acts count more than our subsequent acts. Maybe
seeing forgiveness and repentance as *opposites* is the original mistake.

Ellis maintains that Shakespeare's practical jokes can function to re-
integrate the victims back into the community: "In one distinctly idealistic
notion of how practical jokes should be resolved, the victims are reinte-
grated back into their communities wiser and better people, having learned
important truths about themselves and developed a broader vision of life."[32]
The inclusion of Jonah in the canon suggests that even if Jonah never makes
the move to fully embrace grace, the community may make good Jonah's
legacy. Maybe there is enough bread, contrary to the mother's thoughts in
Goldstein's *Mazel* story.

At inconvenient times, places, and ways, *chus* shows up. Maybe al-
lowing God's mercy to surprise us, not annoy us, is at least as good as any

31. Chesterton, "Whistler," 170.
32. Ellis, *Practical Jokes*, 156.

breast-beating repentance we can muster. Maybe God's audacious compassion is the most practical of God's pranks.

As Eugene Peterson observes, Jonah fails in his disobedience and, sadly, equally fails in his obedience.[33] Jonah is a playful, cautionary tale for sinners, thus suitable for *Yom Kippur*, Lent, and our everyday infringements on God's grace.

33. See Peterson, "Jonah," *Message*, 1664.

Parable of the Potter

by
David Denny[1]

I am who I am,
not who you have
fashioned me to be
in your selfish thoughts.

Does not the potter
maintain the right
to create as he sees fit,
to make or destroy?

I have shaped a dove
from a lump of wet clay,
dried him in the sun,
then taught him to fly.

Now the dove returns
to the potter and
tells him he was wrong
to give him flight.

Because he despises
the potter's other creations,
he prefers to be dashed
against the rocks.

Who knows the mind
of the potter?
Who can fathom
his intentions?

I am the Lord, your God,
gracious and merciful,
slow to anger,
abounding in steadfast love.

1. Denny, *Man Overboard*, 42–43.

Sol's Sins and the Limits of Grace

(Vignette)

The book of Jonah seems to suggest that God's *chus* (compassion; grace) is infinite. Jonah is a small book but has great big characters: the magnitude of the city, the aggregate of the people, and the opposition to God's ways and God's people are great, *gedolah*. The flora, fauna, seas, and weather are either exotic or supersized. The repentance of the inhabitants of Nineveh is capacious enough to include even the cows (Jonah 3:7–8; 4:11). That is good news indeed.

So, is God's audacious compassion *infinite*—or only *great*? Leszek Kolakowski explores the question of the limits of God's compassion in a short tale, "Solomon, or Men as Gods."[1]

Apparently, Solomon had been acting "frivolously" and had "vexed" Jehovah to the point that God had lost his patience. Solomon's *libido* was overdeveloped, having seven hundred wives and three hundred concubines, which, as at least one person has pointed out, amounts to one thousand mothers-in-law. Most of these wives and concubines worshiped foreign gods. These practices "boiled" Jehovah's indignation—and they were expensive!

Now Solomon had learned in catechism class that God's mercy is "boundless" (*chus*). But at the bottom of Solomon's heart "he really did not believe it."[2] Jehovah sent King Solomon a telegram (they did not have, as yet, the gift of the gods, the Internet!): Cease and desist from this idolatry immediately. Jehovah.

---

1. Kolakowski, *Tales*, 171–79.
2. Kolakowski, *Tales*, 174.

Solomon replied, OK, OK. Solomon.[3]

Of course, nothing changed on the ground. Idols and temples continued to spring up like mushrooms, vile as they are (the mushrooms more so than the idols, according to some sources).

Jehovah sent a second telegram: It seems to me that you consider my patience infinite. Jehovah.

Solomon responded confidently: Yes.

Jehovah's return telegram read: Be advised therefore that you have abused it infinitely. Jehovah.[4]

In the end, perhaps we do well to heed Ellen Davis's observation regarding Jonah: "God desires not only to reclaim the Gentiles but also to have Jonah *as an understanding friend.*"[5]

There is no *necessary* reason to run out of enough bread.

3. Kolakowski, *Tales*, 173.

4. Kolakowski, *Tales*, 174.

5. Davis, *Prophecy*, 53 (emphasis added).

A Tale of Two Women

Diverse elements wrought together in a scrupulous design.

—WALTER NASH, *THE LANGUAGE OF HUMOR*, 25

The brief, often straightforward nature and simplicity of the proverbs in Scripture masks an amazing movement of thought and form, much as jokes have little surprises that often require a second reading to see how the author got from A to B. "A to B" is an apt expression to use with biblical proverbs since most have the structure of two versettes bumping up against one another. These A and B lines may complement one another, extend the thought, or compete with one another. Biblical proverbs play with all the features of language—sound, syntax, semantics, and whatever else the author finds to create dramatic images.

Shapiro says, "Proverbs is a cadenza of prudential severity . . . [actually] it may come closest to a book of dreams or jokes."[1]

Proverbs and jokes feign simplicity but actually require a great deal from us as audience. Yet, even without extensive skill, the casual reader is able to find at least a kernel to savor. As Ellen Davis notes, "The proverbs are spiritual guides for ordinary people, on an ordinary day, when water does not pour forth from rocks and angels do not come to lunch."[2]

Thus, Prov 14:15 reads, "The simple believeth every word: but the prudent man looketh well to his going"(KJV). We probably learned that from our mom or dad: "Don't believe everything you hear." It's rather common sense, which, of course, isn't always so common.

1. Shapiro, "Proverbs," 320.
2. Davis, *Proverbs*, 12.

Much humor has a similar simplicity to it, but also requires from a reader or hearer an ability to move between notions or images. *I think sex is better than logic, but I can't prove it.* This sentence has no special vocabulary but plays off a distinction between merely *thinking* something and being able to *convince* someone of something. One must apprehend two distinct uses of mental faculties intersecting with an arguable physical act.

Most proverbs, as most humor, require some mulling over if we want to move beyond a one-dimensional understanding.

Prov 11:22 says, "As a jewel of gold in a swine's snout, so is a fair woman which is without discretion" (KJV). In the light of our current concerns over certain reductionist portrayals of women, this proverb seems insensitive. Of course our issues were not part of ancient Israel's world. Still, comparing any human to a pig is not likely to go over well if someone feels that it is aimed at said person, female or male.

> If we really want to insult somebody, perhaps we should look to 1 Sam 17:26b, "For who is this uncircumcised Philistine, that he should defy the armies of the living God?" David is not giving wise advice; he is rallying his fellow warriors for the upcoming battle by demeaning this Philistine warrior. I suspect that Goliath is rather thankful that he is not circumcised (but that is another point altogether). An insult may have some wit, but it seldom invites an adjustment opportunity on the part of the victim.

Prov 11:22 connects two images, that of a ring of gold in a swine's snout and that of a fair woman. Michael Fox offers this connection: It is not the swine that lines up with the woman but the "jewel of gold." He cites a more positive view of women in another proverb to show that women are not portrayed universally in a negative light: "A virtuous woman is a crown to her husband" (12:4a). If the wife is without sense, though, that makes the husband of the first proverb the ludicrous person; he is "really strutting about with a preposterous creature."[3]

Davis offers another slant on the proverb, translating the "B" line as, "a beautiful woman, *turned away* from good sense."[4] I'm not sure that either approach "saves" us from the overall image. What both Fox and Davis show, however, is that proverbs, like jokes, require sorting through how

3. Fox, *Proverbs 10–31*, 540.

4. Davis, *Proverbs*, 80. She further comments, "She is not dull-witted but rather flagrantly indiscreet." The verb in question can be translated "turn away."

the images play off one another and what is being advocated or called into question.

We cannot read any of the proverbs specifically speaking about a female without also recognizing that Proverbs is surrounded by women: Lady Wisdom in Prov 1–9 and her incarnation, the Valorous Woman in Prov 31. We also, however, should take into account "Femme Fatale"[5] in Prov 7. That Proverbs takes a singular view of women is simply untenable.

Proverbs are neither commands nor prophecies, but witty observations of common tendencies. As readers we need to explore the wit in the proverb to see precisely what the comparison is rather than settling for a superficial or reductionist solution.

What of humor, then, in Prov 11:22? I would venture to say that the arresting image is "jewelry" on a swine, whether snout or elsewhere. Jesus uses a very similar image in Matt 7:6: "Do not cast your pearls before swine." In both cases it is the incongruity of the image that elicits a smile, if not a chuckle. Jewelry doesn't wear well on pigs.

> "The proverbs in mosaic sharpen one another."
> —Shapiro, "Proverbs," 323

The humorist-author of Proverbs is inviting us to consider our own behavior(s) and whether what we aspire to be is congruent with the values we endeavor to manifest to others. Whether male or female is coincidental to the proverb; there is nothing inherent in either gender that *precludes* such an unflattering comparison.

*

> All the comical inelasticities that Henri Bergson speaks of at the heart of wit are summoned in the images of excess and psychopathology.
>
> —DAVID SHAPIRO, "PROVERBS," 325

Proverbs, glibly glossed:

The glory of youths is their strength,
   but the beauty of the aged is their gray hair. (20:29)

Cold comfort for octogenarians.

---

5. Davis, *Proverbs*, 58–62.

Crush a fool in a mortar with a pestle
    along with crushed grain,
      but the folly will not be driven out. (27:22)

                    Stupid is as stupid does (Forrest Gump).

Whoever digs a pit will fall into it,
    and a stone will come back on the one who starts it rolling. (26:27)

                    What goes around comes around.

Like somebody who takes a passing dog by the ears
    is one who meddles in the quarrel of another. (26:17)

                    First lawyer joke.

Like a maniac who shoots deadly firebrands and arrows,
  so is one who deceives a neighbor
  and says, "I am only joking!" (26:18–19)

                    Hit and run—passive aggressive behavior.

Who has woe? Who has sorrow?
  Who has strife? Who has complaining?
Who has wounds without cause?
  Who has redness of eyes?
Those who linger late over wine,
  those who keep trying mixed wines.
Do not look at wine when it is red,
  when it sparkles in the cup
  and goes down smoothly.
At the last it bites like a serpent,
  and stings like an adder.
Your eyes will see strange things,
  and your mind utter perverse things. (23:29–33)

                    One more for the road, please.

It is better to live in a corner of the housetop
than in a house shared with a contentious wife. (25:24)

Battle of the sexes.

Like a thorn bush brandished by the hand of a drunkard
is a proverb in the mouth of a fool. (26:9)

Sling mud on a wall to see what sticks.

As a door turns on its hinges,
so does a lazy person in bed. (26:14)

"Tossin and Turnin"[6]

The heart knows its own bitterness,
and no stranger shares its joy. (14:1)

A proverb for introverts.

⋆

The world is to be decoded by the most strenuous deciphering, and
the beginning is reverential anxiety.

—DAVID SHAPIRO, "PROVERBS," 315

There is at least one proverb that troubles most sensibilities:

As legs hang limp on a cripple
so is a proverb in the mouth of dullards. (26:7, JPS)

It's easy to read this proverb as a comparison between a person crippled
and "dullards" (foolish; stupid). "Cripple" has become a derogatory term,
very offensive to many people. Hence NRSV has opted for a less offensive
translation:

---

6. A song written by Richie Adams and Malou Rene, featured in the movie *Animal
House.*

The legs of a disabled person hang limp;
so does a proverb in the mouth of a fool. (26:7)

OED *traces the use of the word "cripple" back at least to a translation of Luke 5:24 where Jesus heals the paralytic. The* Vulgate *of Lk 5:24 uses the term* paralytico *from which we get our term "paralytic." The* Vulgate *of Ps 26:5 reads* claudus tibias: *a "halting/lame (shin) bone." The predecessor to* NRSV *reads, "Like a lame man's legs, which hang useless / is a proverb in the mouth of fools" (*RSV*).*

As Auerbach noted years ago, biblical texts do not seek to flatter and please us, but to hold us accountable.[7] The images of the proverbs are often visceral, intended to engage and even disturb us. For example, in Proverbs 9, we are warned about Dame Folly ("Femme Fatale"):

She sits at the door of her house . . .
calling to those who pass by . . .
"Whoever is simple, let him turn in here!"
And to him who is without sense she says,
"Stolen water is sweet,
and bread eaten in secret is pleasant."
But he does not know that the dead are there,
that her guests are in the depths of Sheol.
(Prov 9:14–18)

Proverb 26:7 testifies that "reading is vascular or nothing," as David Shapiro says.[8] These condensed little poems seem simple on the surface but can ruffle readers with odd phrasing or vivid imagery. Poetry and proverbs, maxims, parables, and so forth seek to use language that is visceral and engaging .

If so, Prov 26:7 may be more *descriptive* than offensive. The legs evoked "dangle" or are palsied, perhaps. An "accident" of birth or circumstances?

Whereas the "fool" is precisely, *intentionally*, maybe even stubbornly ignorant: "How long, O simple ones, will you love being simple? / How long will scoffers delight in their scoffing / and fools hate knowledge?" (Prov 1:22). And, "Like snow in summer or rain in harvest / so honor is not fitting for a fool" (Prov 26:1).

Proverbs are not inherently and deliberately attacking a *specific* person so much as an *attribute* that any person may display on occasion. In joke language it is the *behavior* that is the primary focus of the joke, not the person *per se*. If the proverb is apt, it is because the person in question is

---

7. Auerbach, *Mimesis*, 15, says that Homer seeks to flatter and enchant us whereas the biblical text seeks to "subject us."

8. Shapiro, "Proverbs," 327.

displaying certain attributes that are incongruous with normally accepted actions in a particular situation.[9]

The note that accompanies the JPS translation of Prov 26:7 states, "The *dullard* is a verbal cripple." This translation, rightly, focuses the denigration at the "dullard," the foolishness of the person rather than the physical capacities. "He's as dumb as a doorknob" we might say.[10]

Eugene Peterson, in *The Message*, takes what might be the most prudent approach to this proverb, catching both the flavor of it and the force:

> A proverb quoted by fools
> is limp as a wet noodle. (Prov 26:7)

> *"[Proverbs] is an eruptive text of a restless shrewdness that does more than balance the idealism of priests and prophets with the cunning of the 'elders.' . . . [Proverbs contain] a tone of strenuous searching . . ."*
> —Shapiro, "Proverbs," 320

The book of Proverbs is not so much a moralistic scribal textbook as a "whimsical collage of popular art."[11] Humor in Proverbs is generally not spiteful or malevolent. It is not employed as a blunt instrument, but as an invitation to examine one's persona in a given situation.

*

> And we need this fool . . . just as old kings in medieval courts needed fools: because only fools dared to tell them the truth, only fools dared to puncture their vanity.
>
> —A. N. WILSON, *THE VICAR OF SORROWS*, 389

The self-confident king of Proverbs ("Solomon") turns upon himself in Ecclesiastes.

---

9. Swabey observes, "Mockery makes fun of its object through analogy and distortion, while the laughable effect adheres primarily to the depiction, and only secondarily to the original" (Swabey, *Comic Laughter*, 40).

10. Swabey makes an observation that might speak to our unease regarding comments that seem to denigrate physical limitations and the like. She appeals to the effect of the "naturalism of our day" that proposes a "nonsense of an entirely senseless sort" or "cruelty [and] brutality." She locates such appeals to the "stimulus-response mechanism" of laughter that disregards laughter's meaning, and the "natural egotism of the human animal, which gains a feeling of superiority from spiteful criticism and the infliction of pain with anesthesia of the heart increasing proportionately" (Swabey, *Comic Laughter*, 16). That's quite a mouthful, but she seems to be putting the onus on the changing conception of humor and its role in everyday life.

11. Shapiro, "Proverbs," 327.

The Preacher—*Qohelet*—says, "All is vanity . . . all words/things are wearisome" (Eccl 1:2, 8). "Ephemerality and mortality is Qohelet's central theme."[12] Qohelet is not the confident prophet but the ruminative sage. He is not a Stoic, unmoved by the vicissitudes of life, but the one who seems always to respond with, "Yes, but . . . ." Qohelet is "agitated by thoughts that run throughout eternity."[13]

Davis points out that Ecclesiastes is a favored book for ascetics and is read on Sukkot ("Tabernacles") in the Jewish festal calendar when Jews remember their sojourn in the desert after the deliverance from slavery in Egypt.[14] Ecclesiastes is a book for questioners, not the self-satisfied.

In his quest, Qohelet looks at the cosmos and can even sound like a Greek philosopher who sees the world as a "ceaseless monotonous round"[15]:

> A generation goes, and a generation comes . . .
> The sun rises and the sun goes down,
>   and *hurries* to the place where it rises . . .
> *round and round* goes the wind . . .
> All streams run to the sea,
>   but the sea *is not full* . . .
> All things are wearisome . . .
> the eye is not satisfied with seeing,
>   or the ear filled with hearing.
> What has been is what will be . . .
>   there is *nothing new under the sun.*
> Is there a thing of which it is said,
>   "See, this is new"?
> It has already been,
>   in the ages before us.
> The people of long ago are not remembered,
>   *nor will there be any remembrance*
> *of people yet to come*
>   by those who come after them. (Eccl 1:4–11)

---

12. Davis, *Opening*, 342.
13. Fisch, *Poetry*, 164.
14. Davis, *Opening*, 342.
15. Fisch, *Poetry*, 166.

This is not the author of Ps 98 speaking here where creation resounds with song and joy. Fisch says that this notion of world and natural cycles has never more been more graphically formulated—and "never before have the utter hopelessness and wearisomeness of such conceptions been so vividly rendered."[16]

Fisch calls this "spiritual claustrophobia"; Qohelet's "negations demand also to be negated."[17]

These negations come, in part at least, when Qohelet says, "Go, eat your bread with enjoyment, and drink your wine with a merry heart; for God has long ago approved what you do. Let your garments always be white; do not let oil be lacking on your head. Enjoy life with the wife whom you love, all the days of your vain life that are given you under the sun, because that is your portion in life and in your toil at which you toil under the sun. Whatever your hand finds to do, do with your might; for there is no work or thought or knowledge or wisdom in Sheol, to which you are going . . . *time and chance happen to them all*" (Eccl 9:7–10).

> *Even though Qohelet is agitated by eternal thoughts, Fisch notes, "If we only could be satisfied (Pater-like) with moments of grace in which everything is beautiful" (citing Eccl 3:11, "He hath made every thing beautiful in his time" [KJV]; Fisch,* Poetry, *164). Buechner echoes these thoughts when he says, "For all its great beauty, this is a stormy world we live," followed a few pages later by, "Even though there are many other moments when grace seems far away, those moments of grace remain their richest treasure and dearest hope" (Buechner,* Longing for Home, *164, 176).*

*

Why are our days numbered and not, say, lettered?

—WOODY ALLEN

Fisch calls attention to other authors who employ irony to make sense of these vicissitudes and contradictions in life. It has yielded a comic form in Western literature. Qohelet doesn't quite fit this mold in as much as

16. Fisch, *Poetry*, 167.

17. Fisch, *Poetry*, 167.

he affirms that "God will judge the righteous and the wicked, for he has appointed a time for every matter, and for every work" (Eccl 3:17). Fisch sees here a playfulness in Qohelet's thoughts: "This skeptical rejection of skepticism is the final twist" of Qohelet's irony.[18] "To you I'm an atheist; to God, I'm the Loyal Opposition," says Woody Allen in the movie *Stardust Memories*.[19]

*

In *Opening Israel's Scripture*, Ellen Davis titles her section on Ecclesiastes "Living with Death."[20] Ecclesiastes 12 says, "Remember your creator in the days of your youth, before the days of trouble come . . . before the sun and the light and the moon and the stars are darkened . . . and those who look through the windows see dimly . . . when the doors on the street are shut . . . when one is afraid of heights . . . the grasshopper drags itself along and desire fails . . . the pitcher is broken at the fountain, and the wheel broken at the cistern, and the dust returns to the earth as it was, and the breath returns to God who gave it. The end of the matter; all has been heard . . . all is vanity" (Eccl 12:1–8).

"Never was there a gentler poem on the approach of death," Fisch contends, and goes on to say, "What counts is the life given to us, the remembering, the testimony."[21] "Fear God, and keep his commandments; for that is the whole duty of everyone," Qohelet says (Eccl 12:13). Davis, drawing upon Martin Luther, says that these verses serve to cultivate a "capacity for gratitude."[22]

*

> I should stop ruining my life searching for answers
> I'm never gonna get, and just enjoy it while it lasts.

—ELLIOT (WOODY ALLEN), IN *HANNAH AND HER SISTERS*

Qohelet ends his book with an imperative: "*Remember . . .*" (Eccl 12:1). He doesn't say this with the angst and urgency with which Woody Allen's

18. Fisch, *Poetry*, 175.

19. Allen, *Stardust Memories*.

20. Davis, *Opening*, 341.

21. Fisch, *Poetry*, 177–78.

22. Davis, *Opening*, 343.

characters usually speak; rather, he says it more with a sigh. Fox translates this word as *appreciate*: "Appreciate your Creator." Fox also connects this passage to the earlier words in Eccl 11:9b, "Know well that God will call you to account for all such things." Fox further observes, "Both sentences counterbalance the advice to enjoy life with an admonition to remember that God is watching over your acts."[23]

Childs says that memory is a grasping after, a meditating upon, and even a prayer.[24] When in exile the people remembered Zion—and wept (Ps 137:1); when they were restored, laughter and joy ensued (Ps 126:2). In between those experiences, God also remembers: "For he knows how we were made; he remembers that we are dust" (Ps 103:14).

> *Qohelet's words have been read differently by different people over the years. This is the fate of poets who speak words "slant."[25] Bob Dylan's song "Death is not the End" speaks of crossroads we don't comprehend or dreams that have vanished, but also of a tree of life that grows and bright lights that shine in dark, empty skies. The refrain, "Death is not the end" occurs, drumbeat fashion, throughout. Is it a dirge or a faintly hopeful song? Is the emphasis on "death" or "not the end"?*

Peterson in *The Message* renders Qohelet's last words with his characteristic vividness:

> Honor and enjoy your Creator while you're still young,
> Before the years take their toll and your vigor wanes,
> Before your vision dims and the world blurs
> And the winter years keep you close to the fire.
> In old age, your body no longer serves you so well.
> Muscles slacken, grip weakens, joints stiffen.
> The shades are pulled down on the world.
> You can't come and go at will. Things grind to a halt.
> The hum of the household fades away.
> You are wakened now by bird-song.
> Hikes to the mountains are a thing of the past.
> Even a stroll down the road has its terrors.
> Your hair turns apple-blossom white,
> Adorning a fragile and impotent matchstick body.

23. Michael Fox, "Ecclesiastes," in Berlin and Brettler, *Jewish Study Bible*, 78.

24. Childs, *Memory*, 65.

25. Emily Dickenson has that wonderful line, "Tell the truth, but tell it slant."

Yes, you're well on your way to eternal rest,
While your friends make plans for your funeral.
(Eccl 12:2–5, *The Message*)

Gordis relates a homiletic point made by Rabbi Akiva (ca 50–135 C.E.): We are to remember from where we came ("your source"), where you are going ("your grave"), and before whom you will give account ("your Creator").[26]

"Remember" is one of the most important words in all of Scripture both in terms of the number of times it is used and in its particular uses. To remember is to be open to an adjustment opportunity.

The Wisdom tradition is chockful of adjustment opportunities.

26. Gordis, *Koheleth*, 341.

Don't Drink and Decree

Humour therefore consists in the momentary transformation of the
physical into the mechanic, when the mechanic encrusts itself onto
the living, like plaque on the surface of a tooth.

—SIMON CRITCHLEY (EXPLAINING BERGSON), *ON HUMOUR*, 56

Decrees are meant to be followed. This is especially true in Esther's time
when Ahasuerus's empire stretched from east to west with over one
hundred and twenty provinces, and if one has wealth enough to throw a
six-month party. Ahasuerus lacked no land, wealth, or power. That is the
theory anyway.

The festivities create opportunities to ease the burdens of necessity for
running a huge empire. Yet even in the midst of festivities, a potentate must
preserve certain lines of demarcation. On the occasion of this festivity royal
wine flowed freely and the one line of demarcation for drinking was "no
restrictions." A reader might detect a wink from the author that the first
decree is a law without limits. Wine attenuates
reason. A tipsy potentate ought to cause both
characters and readers to be alert.[1]

*"Be Alert!—the world
needs more lerts!"
—Wisdom found on a
bathroom mirror*

The festive occasion deteriorates swiftly in
what Adele Berlin calls the "Vashti Incident."
On the seventh day of the festivities, when the
king is "merry with wine," Ahasuerus instructs
his seven eunuchs to bring in the queen so everybody can admire her. The
author underscores her beauty by telling us that Queen Vashti is *very fine
looking* (Esth 1:11b).

---

1. Berlin, *Esther*, 10.

The eunuchs are told that Queen Vashti is to wear her royal diadem for this occasion. Earlier in the story we are given elaborate details of this festive occasion (Esth 1:6–7). Here the eunuchs are all named, with tongue-twisting names, likely enhancing comic effect: "Indeed, we can picture a troop of eunuchs, in dress uniform, marching in step to fetch the queen.[2] Yet the queen is given little mention apart from her beauty and her royal diadem (Esth 1:11); no other finery is specified. The mention of the diadem alone for Queen Vashti leaves much to a reader's imagination. This absence led some rabbis to opine that Vashti was adorned *solely* with the diadem.[3] Oh my!

> "Chapter 1 sets the tone of the book, and it is a tone of excess, buffoonery, and bawdiness . . . and with a hint of mockery so at home in burlesque."
> —Berlin, Esther, 3

Whether fully clothed or not, Queen Vashti is defiant (Esth 1:12a). The king is incensed by this refusal; indeed he is "burning mad" (Esth 1:12b). The king turns to those who were versed in decrees,[4] his seven closest ministers (Esth 1:14). The ministers warn that Vashti has acted not only against the king, but against *all* the officials and *all* the peoples in *all* the provinces (Esth 1:16). The upshot of Vashti's behavior will be that *all* the wives will despise their husbands and there will be *no end* to the scorn and provocation (Esth 1:17–18). Berlin says, "A domestic incident has become a national crisis."[5]

What to do? Issue a decree—one that, of course, cannot be abrogated (Esth 1:19).

The men, well-versed in decrees and discernment, assure the king that a decree banning Queen Vashti from his court will ensure that *all* the wives will treat their husbands (high and low) with respect (Esth 1:20).

Dispatches are sent out to *every* province, *every* nation in its own language, that *every* man wield authority in his home (Esth 1:22). That last phrase, that every man will be given freedom to wield authority in his own home, prompts this comment by Berlin: "But, as many scholars have

---

2. Berlin, *Esther*, 14.

3. Berlin, *Esther*, 14.

4. The Hebrew has a nice, concise wordplay here to describe the qualities of the ministers: *dat v-din*; they are skilled in "decree and discernment."

5. Berlin, *Esther*, 17.

seen, such an edict is unenforceable, if not downright *silly*, even in a farce."[6] Swabey says in another context, "Simplified generalities are much easier to grasp and 'rib' than individuals in their rich complexity."[7]

With Vashti dispatched, the king issues another decree: find a replacement queen. Enter Esther—and a host of women who are lavished with oodles of cosmetics, six months of myrrh, and six months of perfume (Esth 2:12)!

*

> But the most grave and dreadful things in the world are the oldest
> jokes in the world—being married, being hanged.
> —G. K. CHESTERTON, "HERETICS," 158

The "Vashti Incident" is behind the king. Life at court sans Vashti continues much as before. Decrees need to be made and appointments rendered. Empires run best as well-oiled machines.

Enter Haman. Haman is given a place of honor; he is "promoted . . . advanced . . . and seated higher" than any other officials (Esth 3:2). All the people bow before this courtier, except one. Day after day, Mordecai neither kneels nor bows. People begin to talk. "Why don't you bow, Mordecai?" "I'm a Jew," he answers (Esth 3:1–6). Sand trickles into the well-oiled machine.

Haman is clever in that devious way of people who want power but maybe don't have the charismatic gifts to acquire power except through scheming. He doesn't attack Mordecai directly. Rather, he appeals to the king on legal grounds and on the vanity of the king: "O King, there is a people in your lands whose laws differ from other people's laws—including yours. . . . It is not in your interest to let them rest" (Esth 3:8).

This "Mordecai Incident" turns a single exception into a "national conflict"[8] much as the Vashti incident affected all the wives and their husbands. Mordecai's failure to bow to Haman will affect all of Mordecai's people throughout the kingdom (Esth 3:6).

This national incident seems also to have a history underlying it. Haman, we are told, is an "Agagite" (Esth 3:1). In 1 Sam 15 King Agag of the

6. Berlin, *Esther*, 20 (emphasis added).

7. Swabey, *Comic Laughter*, 34.

8. Berlin, *Esther*, 14.

Amalekites is defeated by King Saul. This attack was carried out because of "what the Amalekites did to Israel when they journeyed back from Egypt" (1 Sam 1:2). Berlin suggests that his reference may even go back to the rivalry between Jacob and Esau (Gen 36:12). This is not just a personal vendetta but one that spans generations, much as the famed Hatfield-McCoy feud.

On the surface, though, it is enough to note that "Mordecai does not accord Haman the honor that is officially due him."[9] Haman "disdains" Mordecai (Esth 3:6). This also echoes Memucan's concern in Esth 1:17 when Queen Vashti refuses to obey Ahasuerus's decree and it is feared that "*all* the wives throughout *all* the empire" will show contempt for their husbands. Potentates can handle most anything except having their signs of authority—their "scepters"—slighted.

To seal the deal with the king regarding the Jews, Haman offers some personal financial compensation: "I will pay ten thousand talents of silver to the royal treasury" (Esth 3:9; does money cover a multitude of bad policies?). The king, surprisingly, refuses the offer of money, but still gives Haman free reign to deal with the Jews. Why does the king refuse Haman's offer? Berlin offers that the king may not be getting much from the Jews anyway so it's not much of a financial loss. More likely might be a continuation of the king's generosity which, like everything else in the book, gets exaggerated.[10]

Extravagance rules this empire. When the decree is sent to all the provinces it stipulates that all the Jews, "young and old, children and women," are to be exterminated. Even the time period to carry out such a task is extravagant in its shortness, *on a single day* (Esth 3:13).

With this new decree, it is time to uncork the bottles again: "The king and Haman sat down for a feast" (Esth 3:15).

*

He always reasons rightly, as madmen do, from his own premises.

—JAMES RUSSELL LOWELL, "HUMOR, WIT, FUN, AND SATIRE," 59

"[Chapter 4] is a somber chapter."[11] All the pageantry is gone. We're in the world of sackcloth, not silk; tears of sorrow, not wine and laughter.

---

9. Berlin, *Esther*, 14.

10. Berlin, *Esther*, 14.

11. Berlin, *Esther*, 40.

Even the language of this chapter has changed from adjectives and adverbs to the more usual prose of Hebrew Scriptures. Auerbach says that Hebrew narrative does not seek so much to flatter us as bewitch us with only as much detail as is necessary to draw us into a future that is "fraught with background."[12] Berlin makes this observation: "God is most present and most absent in this chapter . . . It is hard to read about fasting, mourning, and crying out without seeing God as the addressee."[13]

Mordecai, in sackcloth and ashes, laments outside the city walls, "for no one might enter the king's gate clothed with sackcloth" (Esth 4:2). Esther learns of this and sends a eunuch, Hathach, to enquire of Mordecai. Mordecai sends Hathach back to Esther with a copy of the decree, asking that Esther might intervene on behalf of the Jewish people throughout the provinces. Esther responds with her concern that no one can come into the king's court unless the king extend the royal scepter. Mordecai presses the gravity of his words by pointing out that no Jew, her family included, will escape this edict if she doesn't intervene: "For if you keep silence at such a time as this, relief and deliverance will rise for the Jews from another quarter, but you and your father's family will perish" (Esth 4:14a).

Berlin makes the observation that Mordecai's logic is deficient here, but it's the rhetoric that counts.[14] *We're all in danger, you and your family included.* The point is taken.

When Mordecai is confronted with royal decrees that cannot, *must not*, be abrogated, his "theo-logical" recourse is to *improvise*: "Who knows? Perhaps you have come to royal dignity for just such a time as this" (Esth 4:14b). Mordecai adapts, adjusts, and seeks to overcome.[15]

Esther responds by calling all the Jews in Susa to a three-day fast on her account; "I and my maids will also fast as you do. After that I will go to the king, though it is against the law; and if I perish, I perish" (Esth 4:16). Rather than a feast, as elsewhere in the book, a fast is called. Not despair, but improvisation.

---

12. See Auerbach, *Mimesis*, 3–23.

13. Berlin, *Esther*, 44.

14. Berlin, *Esther*, 49.

15. In the 1986 movie *Heartbreak Ridge*, Clint Eastwood plays a crusty old Marine Gunnery Sergeant, "Gunny Highway." He instructs his young Marines to *adapt, adjust, and overcome* when confronted with seemingly insurmountable obstacles.

Resourceful Esther is ready to go against the law in a land where law rules.[16] She does so, however, within her people's tradition of life before the Lord of the universe. Fasting is a *theological* practice of giving God the space to work in our lives.[17]

> "What I am suggesting, by contrast, is that the only given is God's story, the theo-drama, the church's narrative: all else is potentially gift . . . Ethics is done by people who are on the receiving end, working out how to accept things that present themselves as givens but cannot be since there is only one given— the narrative of Scripture and the church's tradition."
> —*Wells, Improvisation,* 125–26

In chapter 5 Esther dresses royally to meet with the king; "Esther the beauty queen [gives way] to Esther the true queen."[18] The king notices, however, that something is amiss: "What troubles you?"[19] He even offers up to half his kingdom to quell her worry. Esther sidetracks the offer and invites the king to a feast— one already prepared *for him* (Esth 5:4), emphasizing the gift-nature of this event.

Before the banquet occurs, though, a few things transpire between the two adversaries, Haman and Mordecai. Haman is thrilled to be invited to this very exclusive party by Queen Esther. However, a cloud hangs over him when he, once more, sees Mordecai at the palace gate, and Mordecai does not "rise or stir."[20] To his credit Haman "controls himself" on this occasion. He must first go home to tell family and friends of his good fortune, his advancement, his wealth, and especially the queen's feast (Esth 5:9–12). All this good fortune, however, does not compare to Mordecai's public disrespect of Haman (Esth 5:13).

Haman's wife and his friends devise an elaborate plan. If farce has not been evident so far in the book it surely shows its face at this point. This elaborate plan brings to the forefront Henri Bergson's notions of humor where the "physical becomes mechanical." The plan devised is outrageous

16. Berlin, *Esther,* 50.

17. The fast opens a way for the story to continue, not end in death. This is a pattern that runs throughout Scripture and liturgy: fasting then feasting; wilderness then the promised land; Lent then Easter.

18. Berlin, *Esther,* 52, citing Jon Levenson's commentary on Esther.

19. Hebrew *Mah-lak,* "What is it to you?"

20. "Neither rose nor blinked" (5:13).

and inevitably bound to fail, even if God were not to intervene. More often than not, the roadrunner is too fast and nimble for the coyote.

However absent God has (seemingly) been up to this point, Berlin notes that in chapter 4 the author is "hard pressed to write God out of the story."[21]

*

> Actually, our comic amusement is often induced . . . by the discovery of people's unexpected resourcefulness, their nimble alertness, and feats of catlike agility in adjustment.
>
> —A. J. A. WALDOCK, *PARADISE LOST AND ITS CRITICS*, 91–92

The author of Esther may be hard pressed to write God out of the story; God is also not eager to jump into the story and do "special effects" like he does with Moses in Egypt. The characters drive the story. However, God is not *deus ex absentia*, an entirely absent God, in Esther either.

The world of royal courts and finery is where God seems most absent, whereas when we enter the world of Mordecai we find someone who adopted a child whose parents had died; he is on the outskirts

Road Runner, a justifiably famous, long-running cartoon, pits a roadrunner against a coyote. Roadrunners—as their name attests—are fast, reaching speeds of over twenty miles per hour, which is still about half that of a coyote. Roadrunners are also highly adaptable in the harshness of the desert, even adapting to catch and digest poisonous animals, and they work in tandem to catch and swallow rattlesnakes. Coyotes are noted for their adaptability and versatility. They are trickster figures in Native American cultures, often employing deception to gain prey. In the cartoon, Wile E. Coyote devises elaborate traps, usually some mechanical appliance of sorts, rather than use his natural canine skills. Wile E.'s traps inevitably fail. In chasing Roadrunner, Wile E. often slams into a "false" opening in a path, or slides off a cliff, where he spirals down until he disappears, resulting in a little cloud puff that signals that he has hit the ground. They both always live, to chase on another day.

21. Berlin, *Esther*, 44.

of the courts (Esth 2:11), often sits at the city gates (Esth 2:19), refuses to pay homage to Haman, neither rises nor trembles before him (Esth 3:3, 5; 5:9), laments the fate of his people (Esth 4:1, 4), and even when honored by the king, returns to the gate after an obligatory fanfare (Esth 6:12). It is in the final two chapters that Mordecai rises to power, and he does so only through his self-giving efforts to save his people, the Jews (Esth 8–9).

Auerbach makes the point that in Scripture God is most present in the domestic and commonplace. "The sublime influence of God . . . reaches so deeply into the everyday that the two realms of the sublime and the everyday are not only actually unseparated but basically inseparable."[22] Mordecai gets most of his work done sitting at the gate not in the royal palace.

Chapter 5 opens with Esther carrying out her plan for a party. Esther puts on her finest apparel and stands at the entrance of the king's palace—where he can get a good look at her. The king extends his royal scepter, inviting her into his presence (Esth 5:1–2). In this chapter, "Esther shows her courage and her cleverness even more than before."[23] Esther is not deterred by the fact that she could lose her life.

"I am not, of course, suggesting that the text ever explicitly mentions royal impotence, but the comic specter of the idea may well be raised. . . . [It may confirm that] Ahasuerus is a man with a shaky scepter." —Alter, Biblical Narrative, 32

Festive occasions in *Esther*, though, seem to spawn large crises. This is a very different party, only a few select guests; the king and Haman are specifically invited by Esther. The result will be the same: a crisis of epic proportions will follow. Nothing like a bit of drama to make a royal party memorable.

Mordecai has a cameo simply to remind us—and Haman—that he is still there, quietly *ignoring* the ignoble Haman. Haman hates to be ignored; Mordecai's total indifference to Haman causes fury once again (Esth 5:9).

"Every cloud has a silver lining" gets inverted by Haman. For all his elation at this new honor, wealth, and invitation to Esther's private party, Haman simply must share his utter frustration at the "Jew Mordecai" having the gall to simply *sit* while he passes by (Esth 5:13). Haman's wife, Zeresh,

22. Auerbach, *Mimesis*, 22–23.
23. Berlin, *Esther*, 50.

and his friends concoct an elaborate plot to rid Haman of Mordecai forever: build a tower to reach the sky and impale Mordecai upon it (Esth 5:14).

Chapter 6 delays the denouement with a sleepless night by the king. The narration of this scene brings to light Mordecai's past work to save the king's life. Moreover, Haman's mistaken understanding that the king is speaking of him when queried what should be done to a person whom the king desires to honor is wittily wrought. Haman replies that such a person should get everything, including the moon; more specifically, this person should receive a royal garment, a royal horse, and a parade through the city (Esth 6:1–9).

The quickness and force of the response of the king couldn't be greater: "Get going with the garment, the horse, as you have said, and give it to Mordecai, the Jew, who sits at the gate of the king, let nothing drop from what you have said!" (Esth 6:10). "Haman's words come back to haunt him," Berlin observes.[25]

> Berlin points out that this fifty cubit tower is something like a seven-story building—all in Haman's backyard! How to raise Mordecai up there seems not to have crossed their minds. Furthermore, could anyone see Mordecai up that high anyway? A tradition is found in the Midrash Abba Gorion that several trees were called before the Holy One Blessed be He to offer their sacrifice. All the trees offered their signature feature as a suitable sacrifice. However, it was the thorn tree who noted that God is not swayed by bias or bribery, and that since he had no special feature, he would sacrifice himself to "hang this impure man [Haman]."[24]

Berlin points out a midrashic tale whereby the daughter of Haman saw a man leading a royally robed man on horse. She mistook the walking man to be Mordecai and the seated man to be her father. Seizing the moment, she hurls the contents of a chamber pot on the head of the walking man—her father! Berlin further notes that such humor is not all that unusual, showing up in Greek literature and art, and in Rabelais as a normal

---

24. Shemesh, "Flaxseed," 163–64.

25. Berlin, *Esther*, 62. Berlin also notes that some of the *midrashim* add that Haman was obliged to act as Mordecai's personal servant.

part of "carnivalesque" literature.[26] Boys of all times and ages will be boys apparently, even if it is a daughter.

"If there was any doubt about the comic nature of the Book of Esther, it is completely dispelled in this chapter [Esth 6], one of the funniest anywhere in the Bible. The plot is constructed on coincidence, misunderstanding, and reversal."[27]

∗

> Tanner's [a character in Flannery O'Connor's story "Judgment Day"] grisly death is yet another validation of O'Connor's witty analysis at work: while lots of folks get killed, nobody gets hurt.
>
> —RALPH WOOD, *FLANNERY O'CONNOR*, 141

Plotting, deception, institutional violence and death are ever-present in Esther. Yet nobody ever really gets hurt.

That's not exactly true, Haman gets *impaled*, but does so on the device of his own making for his archrival, Mordecai. Haman's impaling is more like cartoon violence; it is retributive justice. Wile E. Coyote comes back by the next episode, doesn't he? Haman is a stock villain, we might conclude.[28]

"Cartoon" is a bit of a stretch, but if one reads the literature on Esther, one would find various aspects of the book or some events in the book described as farce, slapstick, burlesque, comic and carnival, hilarity, humor, ridiculous, parody, playful, silly, revelry . . . just to name a few.

After Haman's death and his edict is revoked, we read that the "Jews experienced light and joy, merriment and honor . . . drinking and festivities . . ." (Esth 8:16–17). Amid the ever-present prospect of danger and death, Esther itself falls on the side of the carnivalesque nature of the story.

> *Brief explanation of every Jewish Festival: They attacked us. We won. Let's eat.*

More importantly, we see the key figures in the story *improvising*—accepting, blocking, over-accepting—in response to

---

26. Berlin, *Esther*, 63.

27. Berlin, *Esther*, 56.

28. I suppose we could say that Haman comes back every year at Purim, the festival that celebrates the Jews surviving exilic persecution. Small comfort for him, though he did seem to seek notoriety. Be careful what you pray for!

the actions of the characters and the events and themes that arise from each response through uses of power, edicts, plotting, status, and so forth. The legalism of the empire lacks agility and plays bad for nearly everyone, mostly blocking options. Mordecai and Esther, however, are nimble throughout the story, seeking grace in a largely grace-less situation ("accepting" the offer, but doing so in the creative ways Wells calls "over-accepting"). As Mordecai says, "For if you surely hold your peace at this time, relief and deliverance *may* rise for the Jews from another quarter . . ." (Esth 4:14a).

The storyteller employs comic techniques—reversals, mistaken actions and words, overreaction—to give space for the characters to negotiate the vagaries of life. The king and Haman do not act freely because they are bound by their own instituted laws (they seem to lack improvisational skills, being bound by law, customs, and expectations). Mordecai and Esther have more freedom to act since they know the story doesn't have to "come out right" by our individual actions since it is God's prerogative to determine when and how the story ends.[29]

What the book of Esther displays most beyond the individual elements and strategies that comprise humor is the basic structure of narrative humor itself, what Whedbee calls a "U-shaped plot." Whedbee notes that narrative humor works through actions that signal a sudden *downturn* in the fortunes of a character or situation, and then a sudden *upturn* from another action that results in celebration of joy.[30]

Esther is thoroughly comic in the overall shape of the story and in numerous details as the characters act and react to twists and turns of life in exile. It is a *ridiculous* story in the best sense that it causes us to laugh—and nobody really gets hurt! Stories of the reversal of fortunes also serve to shape the identity of a persecuted people.

For all its drama, Esther is quite mirthful and festive. Uncork the wine, please.

---

29. A point made by Wells, *Improvisation*, 128.

30. Whedbee, *Comic Vision*, 5–11; Whedbee notes elements such as "conventional types" (fools, tricksters, rogues, etc.) and characteristic strategies (incongruities, reversals, surprise) that get played in the U-shaped plot.

Let's Drink to That!

(Vignette)

Purim is the Jewish festival associated with Esther. It is celebrated on the fourteenth of Adar (late winter or early spring). It celebrates toppling the plot by the evil Haman to destroy the Jews throughout the Persian Empire (ca. fourth century BCE). It is a festive occasion that entails dressing up (the children especially), plenty of food and alcoholic beverages, and the giving of gifts and charitable donations.

The primary focus of the celebration is the reading of the *Megillah*, the Scroll of Esther. Besides blessings chanted before and after the reading, and the giving of gifts to the poor, there are no other liturgical directions or theological observations.

One tradition of Purim is that one should drink wine until you can't make a distinction between the evil Haman and the righteous Mordecai! Of course, these more riotous traditions lead some to question the religious value of the feast. Ismar Elbogen, a prominent Jewish scholar, comments at the end of his article on Purim, "The noisy disturbances have been eliminated in every *civilized country*."[1] I suspect Mordecai would find this lack of festivity too dour and may choose to sit at the city gate rather than participate.

Harold Fisch suggests another approach. This lack of instruction regarding the practices and customs of Purim, especially the lack of any theological observations in the Mishnah and on the customs of riotous behavior that accompanies this festival, suggests rather that, "to read the scroll says something about memory itself. . . . The book is a sign of God's remembering . . . linking our days, each to each, and all our times and seasons to the mind of God."[2]

1. Elbogen, *Jewish Liturgy*, 110 (emphasis added).
2. Fisch, "Reading," 72.

Irrevocable Decrees Versus the Probity of *Torah*

(Vignette)

Regarding the books of Esther and Daniel, Davis makes this observation, "With deep sense of irony and grim humor, they prompt reflection on the meaning of Jewish existence in the larger sweep of world events across centuries."[1] The meaning of Jewish existence, and the irony and grim humor are never more evident than in the decrees made by King Ahasuerus in Esther and King Nebuchadnezzar in Daniel.

In Dan 2:1 we read that "Nebuchadnezzar dreamed such dreams that his spirit was troubled and his sleep left him." None of the "magicians, the enchanters, the sorcerers, and the Chaldeans" could interpret the dream because it was "too difficult" (Dan 2:11–12). A decree, of course, was issued to execute all of them. Daniel responds with "prudence and discretion to Arioch, the king's chief executioner" asking why the urgency of this matter (Dan 2:14).

Daniel gets an audience with King Nebuchadnezzar and interprets the dream (Dan 2:25–45). All's well . . . until we turn the page. Dan 3 begins with the king making a golden statue that is sixty cubits high (Dan 3:1).[2]

So the king sent for the "satraps, the prefects, and the governors, the counselors, the treasurers, the justices, the magistrates, and all the officials of the provinces" and had the herald proclaim, "You are commanded, O peoples, nations, and languages, that when you hear the sound of the horn, pipe, lyre, trigon, harp, drum, and entire musical ensemble, you are to fall down and worship the golden statue that King Nebuchadnezzar has set up. Whoever does not fall down and worship shall immediately be thrown into a furnace of blazing fire" (Dan 3:3–6).

1. Davis, *Opening*, 376.

2. Recall that the gallows in Esther was only fifty cubits. Is this a classic case of one king saying that his statue is bigger than the other king's gallows?

Shadrach, Meshach, and Abednego said to the king that "our God" is quite capable of delivering us, but even if God chooses not to deliver us, "Be it known to you, O king, that we will not serve your gods and we will not worship the golden statue that you have set up" (Dan 3:17–18).

Seven types of leaders witnessed this event and seven types of musical instruments were used in the fanfare; furthermore the fire was turned up seven times hotter than normal, indeed it was so hot that the servants, who were to throw the three men into the fire, burned up and yet not the three men, not even the hair on their heads was singed (Dan 3:27).

In contrast to law generally, the image of law in Scripture is not so much rule-based as relationship-based: "Surely, this commandment that I am commanding you today is not too hard for you, nor is it too far away. It is not in heaven, that you should say, 'Who will go up to heaven for us, and get it for us so that we may hear it and observe it?' Neither is it beyond the sea, that you should say, 'Who will cross to the other side of the sea for us, and get it for us so that we may hear it and observe it?' No, the word is very near to you; it is in your mouth and in your heart for you to observe" (Deut 30:11–14).

Ellen Davis observes, "Implicit . . . [in this understanding of law is that it] prescribes certain modes of embodied theology and spirituality. In shaping behavior, it also forms certain attitudes and understanding with respect to God and the world as God's creation."[3]

Both Nebuchadnezzar here in Daniel and Ahasuerus in Esther are kings of very powerful empires. They are also portrayed as hapless, if not helpless against the faithfulness—and cleverness!—of the Jewish people in exile. Indeed, the kings themselves become enslaved by their very decrees: "For an edict written in the name of the king and sealed with the king's ring *cannot be revoked*" (Esth 8:8).[4]

The Talmud counts 613 laws in the Pentateuch; included in that count are the "big ten." These laws are meant to be kept, not as abstract eternal decrees, but in the context of *covenantal loyalty* based on what God has done for the people: "You have seen what I did to the Egyptians, and how I bore you on eagles' wings and brought you to myself. Now therefore, if you obey my voice and keep my covenant, you shall be my treasured possession

---

3. Davis, *Opening*, 57.

4. See further Davis, *Opening*, who observes that Darius, unlike Ahasuerus, "recognizes real sovereignty when he sees it," citing Dan 6:25–7 where Darius confesses the "God of Daniel" as the "living God . . . who delivers and rescues."

out of all the peoples. Indeed, the whole earth is mine, but you shall be for me a priestly kingdom and a holy nation" (Exod 19:4–6).

Screech observes, "Where there is free-will there is room for comedy, even at a cosmic level. Synergism provides a rich field for Christian laughter."[5]

---

5. Screech, *Laughter*, 263.

Liquor Is Quicker

(Vignette)

Candy / is dandy / but liquor / is quicker.

—OGDEN NASH, "ICE BREAKING"

The first mention of drinking an alcoholic beverage comes very early on in Scripture. After the flood, Noah planted a vineyard, harvested the grapes, made wines—and got drunk (Gen 9:20–21).

Long before the folk music revival in the 1950s and 1960s, "kisses sweeter than wine" were intimated in Scripture, "Let him kiss me with the kisses of his mouth! For your love is better than wine" (Song 1:1). It is also a sign of God's blessing: "The mountains shall drip sweet wine, and all the hills shall flow with it" (Amos 9:13b).

Of course, every blessing can turn into a curse when misused: "Wine is a mocker, strong drink a brawler" wisdom tells us (Prov 20:1a).

*

Potentates aren't always known for their wisdom, and drinking has led more than one to make bad decisions. In Dan 5 King Belshazzar held a grand festival. Wine flowed and under the influence of the wine, the king commands that the vessels of gold and silver taken from the temple of the Lord in Jerusalem be used for imbibing the wine for this party they were having. Of course, after a few goblets of wine, they began to praise the gods of gold and silver, among other deities.

Immediately a finger writes on the wall; the king turns "pale" and his knees "knock" together (Dan 5:6). All the king's diviners and all the king's enchanters are unable to interpret the writing. Daniel, however, is remembered by the queen and is summoned to interpret these words. It's not good news for Belshazzar: "Your days are numbered" (Dan 5:26); indeed, the king dies that very night (Dan 5:30).

We saw a similar pattern in Esther when King Ahasuerus gets into trouble whenever he throws a drinking party. He writes checks that he can't cash with his grand decrees. The king's decrees are so wide-ranging that they achieve nothing good for king and kingdom. As Adele Berlin noted, "But, as many scholars have seen, such an edict is unenforceable, if not downright silly, even in a farce."[1]

*

Samson (usually with Delilah) may be one of the most filmed characters in all of Scripture. He even teamed up with Hercules and Ulysses in a 1963 film! "Simply put, there is nothing quite like it [the Samson cycle] in the Bible," Fox says.[2]

In the Samson story we're told that the children of Israel were doing evil in the sight of the Lord (Judg 13:1). Nothing new here, but it does signal that the Lord may initiate a new act. It should also come as no surprise that God chooses a barren woman; that is one of God's favorite *modus operandi*, apparently. God also sends a "messenger" to give the good news. The messenger further gives some instructions, three to be exact: Don't drink wine or beer, don't eat *tamei* (unclean food), and don't cut his hair (Judg 13:7).

When Manoah, the woman's husband, was told of these things, he entreated the Lord to give the couple some instructions as to the child. A messenger was again dispatched, confirming the report of Manoah's wife. Manoah enquires as to the name of the messenger but is rebuffed. Even so, Manoah offers a goat kid to the Lord in thanksgiving. When the fire is lit, the flame went "upward from the altar to the heavens," and the messenger went up with the flame! The awestruck couple flung themselves on the ground (Judg 13:15–21).

They never saw the messenger again.

1. Berlin, *Esther*, 20 (see also this book's chapter "Don't Drink and Decree").

2. Fox, *Early Prophets*, 207.

So begins one of the most incredible and delightful stories in all of Scripture. It is the story of Samson (Judg 13–16).

For our purposes, though, the story told in 1 Judg 14 reinforces the dangers of liquor. Judges 14 begins with a problem. Samson sees a Philistine woman who catches his attention. He must have her; he tells his parents, "So-now, take her for me as a wife!" His parents are concerned, "What?—you have to take a woman from the 'Foreskinned Ones?'" Events unfold, including the killing of a lion, which he tears apart "as one tears apart a kid [goat]." The woman is impressed and, apparently, they married since the father comes a year later to see how things are going. "Shimson[3] made a drinkfest there, *for that is what young men do*" (Judg 14:10).[4]

The party ensues with "thirty feasting-companions." During the party Samson offers a riddle, one nobody can unravel. Samson's wife eventually wheedles it out of Samson and all kinds of havoc ensues, ending—two chapters later—with Samson tearing down the temple of the Philistines and ending his life in the process. The author tells us, "Now the dead whose death he caused at his death were more than those whose death he had caused in his life" (Judg 16:30). Samson was a judge over Israel for twenty years.

*

There is yet another story of a drinking party that goes awry (Matt 14). Herod had imprisoned John the Baptist because John was speaking out about Herod's illegal marriage to Herodias, the wife of his brother Philip. At Herod's birthday party the daughter of Herodias dances before Herod and it pleases him greatly. So Herod grants her whatever she wishes. Prompted by her mother, she replies, "Give me the head of John the Baptist here on a platter." While this request grieves Herod, potentates must save face (Matt 14:9–11).

Warning: consumption of alcoholic beverages can impair your judgment. The humor following heavy drinking seldom has any wit to it. The stories that derive from drinking bouts, however, are often rather clever in their telling. Drinker Beware!

---

3. "Samson" in most English translations.

4. Fox, *Early Prophets*, 217 (emphasis added).

*

Lest we all become teetotalers, the first miracle done by Jesus was at the wedding feast at Cana, in Galilee (John 2). It got high marks: "Everybody I know begins with their finest wines and after the guests have had their fill brings in the cheap stuff. But you've saved the best till now!" (John 2:10, *The Message*). Moreover, there will be wine in abundance in the eschatological kingdom: "The mountains shall drip sweet wine, and all the hills shall flow with it" (Amos 9:13b).

"O drink to thirst, and thirst to drink that measure, Where the only danger is to keep a measure."[5]

Amen.

5. William Alabaster, "Upon the Crucifix (2)," in Smith, *Metaphysical Wit*, 90. See also Story and Gardner, *Sonnets*.

Gods Who Can't God

Laughter and prayer are the two noblest habits of man;
they mark us off from the brutes. To laugh at cheap jests
is as base as to pray to cheap gods.

—CHRISTOPHER MORLEY, *THE HAUNTED BOOKSHOP*, 108

Humor hornswaggles idols.

In the time of the prophet Samuel the Israelites lose a major battle to the Philistines. In response, the elders of Israel bring the ark of the Lord from Shiloh as a kind of talisman to aid them in their battle. The Philistines are deeply troubled by this move for they know the story how the God of the Israelites struck down the Egyptians. Nevertheless they "took courage" and acted "like men," and not only defeated the Israelites, they also took captive the ark of the Lord and installed it as war booty in their own temple to Dagon in Ashdod (1 Sam 4–5).

However, Peterson notes, "God is not a piece of spiritual technology,"[1] as both the people of God and the Philistines seem to treat the ark of God.

The impotence of Dagon gets exposed when the God of Israel plays a practical joke on the Philistines.

In the solitude of the foreign temple at night, God, unbidden and unseen, causes Dagon to topple, not randomly but face down before the coffer of the Lord, as a slave to a master. When the Philistines rise early the next morning, with the intention of worshiping the victorious Dagon, they found Dagon *worshiping* the Lord Almighty.

The Philistines place Dagon back in his original position. The Lord Almighty parries by knocking Dagon down again—and severs Dagon's head and hands. Dagon, headless, handless, has nothing to say and can't do anything since his hands are tied, metaphorically speaking (1 Sam 5:1–4).

---

1. Peterson, *Samuel*, 45.

There is a bit of "magical realism" in this scene where, in the dark of the night, the Lord *duels* Dagon.[2] The Lord Almighty now occupies Dagon's temple with Dagon there only by God's forbearance.

The joke turns more personal when God afflicts the Philistines with an outbreak of tumors on their private parts (1 Sam 5:6), which the King James Version unembarrassedly renders "hemorrhoids."

If this is not bad enough, when the Philistines move the ark of God to nearby Gath, more hemorrhoids follow to those inhabitants—"from small to great" (1 Sam 5:9). The ark gets passed down the road, this time to the inhabitants of Ekron, where, we are told, "the hand of God was very heavy there; those who did not die were stricken with tumors, and the cry of the city went up to heaven" (1 Sam 5:11–12).

> "Overnight the ark, instead of being a prize of war, becomes a hot potato." —Peterson, *Samuel*, 46

After seven months the Philistines return the ark of God to Israel with an offering in hopes of healing: "And they said, 'What is the guilt offering that we shall return to him?' They answered, 'Five gold tumors and five gold mice, according to the number of the lords of the Philistines; for the same plague was upon all of you and upon your lords. So you must make images of your tumors and images of your mice that ravage the land, and give glory to the God of Israel; perhaps he will lighten his hand on you and your gods and your land. Why should you harden your hearts as the Egyptians and Pharaoh hardened their hearts? After he had made fools of them, did they not let the people go, and they departed?'" (1 Sam 6:4–6).

In 1 Sam 6:1–18 the tumors and the mice are mentioned five times; two times mention is made of them being made of "gold." Their affliction obviously made a lasting impression on the people.

Some stories are simply deliciously comic in their telling.

*

[Idolaters] mistake the sign for the reality.
—STEPHEN FOWL, *IDOLATRY*, 8

Humor undercuts not only the idolatry of foreign nations, but also the idolatries among God's own people.

2. Chapman, *Samuel*, 91.

Stephen Fowl maintains that the people of God often turned to worship other gods, but it was rarely a wholesale abandonment. Rather, they made incremental moves, compromises, and slipped into practices that were inimical to worship of the God of Israel. It was "rarely total turning from God."[3] Fowl makes the point that people tend to "lapse into idolatry."[4] The Canadian singer-songwriter Bruce Cockburn has a song that captures that reality, "The Trouble With Normal Is It Always Gets Worse."

Enter Elijah who, as Fox notes, "appears as if from nowhere, mediates miraculous deeds, and inserts the word of Yhwh into the political events of the region."[5] He also grouses before the Lord, "I have had enough, Lord . . . Take my life; I am no better than my ancestors" (1 Kgs 19:9–10).

In 1 Kgs 18 there is a justly famous encounter between Elijah and the prophets of Baal and Asherah, whom the people of Israel are worshiping alongside Yahweh. It takes place on Mt. Carmel, which overlooks the Mediterranean Sea, just south of "Baal country." Elijah, alone, goes against four hundred fifty prophets of Baal and four hundred prophets of Asherah. This, Fox says, is as "theatrical as anything" in the Bible.[6] The issue is which god will bring rain to this horrible drought that has taken place.

Elijah addresses the people, "How long will you hop on two branches?" (1 Kgs 18:21). In a note Fox offers "limp on two crutches" as a possible rendering to capture the image.[7] Having split attention is an apt image for idolatry.

A contest ensues. Two bulls are chosen, one for the prophets of Baal and one for Elijah. They are to set the bulls atop wood piles, but no fire is to be set. Each are to call upon their respective gods and whichever god answers with fire is God (1 Kgs 18:23–24). The prophets of Baal go first, then Elijah.

When the prophets call upon Baal "there was no voice, and no one answering," even though they "hopped" around the altar (1 Kgs 18:26).[8] Elijah, never one to miss a chance or a "dig," instructs them to call louder since their god may be "doing his business" (once again, likely "potty humor"; 1 Kgs 18:27). Fox notes that the scatological interpretation fits the

---

3. Fowl, *Idolatry*, 30.

4. Fowl, *Idolatry*, 9.

5. Fox, *Early Prophets*, 659.

6. Fox, *Early Prophets*, 666.

7. Fox, *Early Prophets*, 670.

8. Fox, *Early Prophets*, 671.

taunt; these gods are subject to the same human necessities as we are.[9] We hear the outcome of this further ranting by the prophets of Baal: "There was no voice, no one answering, and no attention"(1 Kgs 18:29).

Elijah gets his turn now. He builds an altar out of twelve stones, one for each of the twelve tribes of Israel; he digs a trench around the altar big enough to hold a large amount of water—and then he doubles it. If that is not enough, Elijah doubles it again (18:34). Elijah soaks the alter, quite likely to increase the "poke-in-the-eye" humiliation of Baal and his worshipers.

The fire of the Lord falls, consuming the "offering-up and the wood and the stones and the dust and the water that was in the channel it licked up" (1 Kgs 18:38).[10] The altar and the channel go from sopping wet to dry as a bone in one fell swoop.

The victory by Elijah is all the more entertaining since Baal, the storm-god who thunders and brings rain, is mute and dry.

Another instance where idolatry is portrayed humorously is when Moses returns from going up the mountain to get the commandments from God. Moses finds the people worshiping a golden calf. Aaron explains to Moses that the people got worried and thought Moses wasn't returning, so they gathered all their jewelry, threw it in the fire—and out popped the golden calf (Exod 32:21–25). Idols become convenient scapegoats for bad behavior.

*

Who would bother making gods [who] can't "god"?

—ISAIAH 44:10, *THE MESSAGE*

The prophets and poets of ancient Israel go beyond mere humorous stories about idolatry to assail the muddle-headed thinking of idol-making itself. For example, Isaiah portrays the hard work and care that goes into idol-making: First, a workman finds a good tree; then, with a sharp axe, the tree is felled and fashioned into an appropriate shape. Once shaped the tree is trimmed with silver and gold, then nailed so it doesn't "totter." Isaiah continues his detailed account of idol-making, noting the care the ironsmith

9. Fox, *Early Prophets*, 671.

10. Fox, *Early Prophets*, 673.

takes to forge the steel over high heat, neither eating nor drinking all day so he can finish it; then the carpenter uses a stylus, plane, and compass to shape a human-like beauty (Isa 44; cf. also Ps 115).

This passage is a veritable vocabulary lesson for a craftsman. Childs says that these descriptive details "reveal careful firsthand observations."[11] Peterson renders Isa 44:12b (*The Message*), "Such hard work! He works away, fatigued with hunger and thirst." The craftsman is dog-tired fashioning this piece of wood.

Isaiah, a consummate iconoclast and satirist here, destroys all this hard work not with a cudgel but with the scalpel of common sense. In a litany of words again, these associated with discernment, Isaiah says, "They do not *know*, nor do they *comprehend*; for their *eyes are shut*, so that they *cannot see*, and their *minds* as well, so that they *cannot understand*. No one *considers*, nor is there *knowledge* or *discernment* to say, 'Half of it I burned in the fire; I also baked bread on its coals, I roasted meat and have eaten. Now shall I make the rest of it an abomination? Shall I fall down before a block of wood?' He feeds on ashes; a deluded mind has led him astray, and he cannot save himself or say, '*Is not this thing in my right hand a fraud?*'" (Isa 44:18–20, emphasis added).

The idolater fashions the idols with one hand and with the other hand he barbeques his dinner from the same block of wood that formed the idol. He finds no dissonance in these actions. Isaiah would be hard-pressed to call these idolaters *homo sapiens* ("wise humans").

Isaiah exposes these idols by noting that they are devoid of anything that might speak of life or form. They neither see nor know so they will

> "Our God is in heaven
>   doing whatever he wants to do.
> Their gods are metal and wood,
>   handmade in a basement shop:
> Carved mouths that can't talk,
>   painted eyes that can't see,
> Tin ears that can't hear,
>   molded noses that can't smell,
> Hands that can't grasp, feet that can't walk or run,
>   throats that never utter a sound.
> Those who make them have become just like them,
>   have become just like the gods they trust"
> (Ps 115:3–8, The Message).

---

11. Childs, *Isaiah*, 343.

feel no shame. He asks a rhetorical question: "Who would fashion a god or idol that is of no use?" (Isa 44:10).

The tale that comes to mind when I consider these passages is Hans Christian Andersen's "The Emperor's New Clothes." The tale involves a monarch—vain, of course ("vanity" is only cute in a three-year-old grand-daughter!)—who wants to impress everybody with the best suit of clothes ever. The *habiliments* created by the haberdashers exceed the monarch's wildest imagination, literally. It takes a child to point out that the monarch is *au naturel*.

Isaiah's humor questions the obvious that we simply assume and in-vites us to see the obvious that we are not seeing. Idols "can't god."

*

> It is that of a world turned upside down . . . and precisely for that
> reason more revealing of some underlying truths than the conven-
> tional, right-side-up view.
>
> —PETER BERGER, *REDEEMING LAUGHTER*, 21

It is not simply the logic of "bricks and mortar" that trouble the bibli-cal authors, but the logic of the transaction between human and deities that troubles them. It is the logic of "if-then": if I lay an offering at the feet of the idol—a "thing" that I have made with my own hands, from everyday ma-terials—then I will placate (or honor) the gods and reap benefits (whether health, wealth, or some other desired benefit). *Quid pro quo.*

Humor enlists the logic of the absurd; idolatry is simply absurd logic to the biblical authors.

The biblical authors find powerful, sometimes disconcerting images to show the logic of idolatry. One of the more powerful images is that of adultery. Micah likens idolatry to the hires of a prostitute:

> All her images shall be beaten to pieces
> all her wages shall be burned with fire,
> and all her idols I will lay waste;
> for as the wages of a prostitute she gathered them,
> and as the wages of a prostitute they shall again be used. (Mic 1:7)

Similarly, Ezekiel tells an extended parable of the ludicrous nature of the people's idolatry-adultery, even going so far as to say that they are so foolish that they pay their "client" rather than collecting any payment, as is the normal transaction between a client and prostitute. Ezekiel sets forth this scenario:

> *Proverbs warns us,*
> *"For a prostitute is a*
> *deep pit; an adulter-*
> *ess is a narrow well"*
> *(Prov 23:27).*

How weak is thine heart, saith the Lord God, seeing thou doest all these things, the work of an imperious whorish woman; In that thou buildest thine eminent place in the head of every way, and makest thine high place in every street; and hast not been as an harlot, in that thou scornest hire; But as a wife that committeth adultery, which taketh strangers instead of her husband! They give gifts to all whores: but thou givest thy gifts to all thy lovers, and hirest them, that they may come unto thee on every side for thy whoredom. And the contrary is in thee from other women in thy whoredoms, whereas none followeth thee to commit whoredoms: and in that thou givest a reward, and no reward is given unto thee, therefore thou art contrary. (Ezek 16:30–34, KJV)

This snippet from the larger chapter has a comic element in it, but the whole chapter is rather more honest, indeed graphically, brutally so.

Ezekiel 16 is the longest prophecy in the book. Each of its three divisions ends with a "declares the Lord" (affirming divine authorship).[12] Ezekiel's parable begins with the Lord finding an abandoned infant girl whom God raises, watches her grow into a healthy young woman, and eventually pledges a troth to her. Things go "south" from here.

The husband (God) provides for her, even perhaps indulgently (Ezek 16:13). She, however, spends her benefaction on fornication (Ezek 16:15–19); she even sacrifices her children to her idols (Ezek 20–22). She fornicates with "every passer-by" and everybody in the region (Ezek 16:23–34).

The husband lashes out at her, with a detailed and brutal description of what will happen when he hands her over to her lovers (Ezek 16:35–43). Once exposed she may learn shame (Ezek 16:44–58). The diatribe ends with a promise, that the Lord will remember his covenant and forgive all that was done (Ezek 16:59–63).

12. Greenberg, *Ezekiel*, 292.

The parable is long, lurid, and shocking, with unique and rare words, and odd grammatical constructions.[13] There are gibes along the way; even the Philistine women were ashamed of her brazenness (Ezek 16:27). But the vivid imagery and moral outrage are visceral and have caused an equally visceral response by critics.

Ezekiel 16 admittedly does not contain much in the manner of humorous elements.[14] It does expose the idolatry for what it is: faulty in thought, word, and deed—and extremely detrimental to the life of the community of faith. The absurd logic of idolatry is not neutral, but deeply harmful in its effects.

Greenberg notes two themes that run through this extended, detailed story: memory and shame. Israel was to remember the Lord's "redemptive and sustaining deeds . . . as the chief motive of obedience to his commandments."[15] Before we hear whether "she" will remember the Lord's commandments we are told, "I [The Lord] will remember my covenant with you in the days of your youth, and I will establish with you an everlasting covenant" (Ezek 16:60). The Lord first remembers so that *she* can also remember. This parable, Greenberg says, is told to "awaken . . . her memory."[16]

At the risk of skipping over the real and dangerous issues of abuse, Ezekiel is showing us, overly vivid in its details to be sure, the *effects* of idolatry. He is writing to the faithful, those who know the stories, poems, and instructions that defined the people of God. Ezekiel's parable is a grizzly cautionary tale meant to shock, not comfort.

13. Greenberg, *Ezekiel*, 296.

14. If the lurid elements elicit any humor or laughter, it would be a rather dark humor, more disturbing than humorous, and if there be any laughter, it would be joyless and degenerate at best. The image is "grotesque, if not pornographic" (Davis, *Opening*, 303). For an honest, yet theologically helpful discussion of Ezek 16 and its images, see Davis's full discussion where she notes the complex interplay between metaphors, linguistic habits, literary elements, and social situations. She also notes the rhetoric and habits of war, where atrocities are carried largely without impunity and where "antilanguage" may serve to force a counter-reality. Ezekiel does not end his diatribe with abandonment; rather he reminds the people of the Lord's "eternal covenant" (Ezek 16:60–63; Davis, *Opening*, 303–6). The prodigal child is welcomed home.

15. Greenberg, *Ezekiel*, 305.

16. Greenberg, *Ezekiel*, 306. Shockingly so, I would add. "Memory" is one of the key themes that runs throughout Scripture, often calling God's people to covenant loyalty (with its reciprocal commitment). God remembers his covenant with Israel (Exod 2:24); Jesus entreats his followers to remember him by celebrating the Lord's Supper (Luke 22:19).

This material transactional relationship that idolatry offers is a form of folly, but also a betrayal of the *covenant relationship* that God offers. In any relationship there are expectations, to be sure. The expectations of God, however, have more to do with our "dispositions, habits, and practices"[17] than a *tit-for-tat* exchange of material goods. Ezekiel's underlying argument seems to be that idolatry and adultery are two sides of the same coin; they are betrayals of commitment and trust which lead to practices that undermine our deepest relationships.

Another prophet, Hosea, laments (in a drumbeat rhythm): *eyn emet, eyn chesed, eyn da'at.* "There is no truth, there is no mercy, there is no knowledge" (Hos 4:1).[18]

Ezekiel's parable invites the audience to consider actions and outcomes without the pain of living through the experience first. It is an invitation to an adjustment opportunity. Buechner notes that a parable is a "small story with a large point"; the point may be a fun point, but it may contain "sadness" as well.[19]

*

Our understanding is that satire is sneaky, unfair, it takes no prisoners. He knows right from wrong; he has stern morals and leaves bruises.

—GUY DAVENPORT, *THE HUNTER GRACCHUS*, 310

The prophets of Israel show little patience with drivel. In the world of fanatics, a reasonable person is scolded:

---

17. A point Fowl appeals to and develops throughout *Idolatry*; see, e.g., 3–4, *passim*.

18. *Eyn* is the "predication of non-existence" in Hebrew; "There is not (an existence of) . . ." may be a more descriptive translation. Hos 4:2–3 lists some of the outcomes that result from the betrayal of covenant "truth, mercy, and knowledge": "Swearing, lying, and murder, and stealing and adultery break out; bloodshed follows bloodshed. Therefore the land mourns, and all who live in it languish; together with the wild animals, and the birds of the air, even the fish of the sea are perishing." It is not simply the people that suffer, but flora and fauna as well, indeed the whole land (giving a nod to Lev 18:28: "Otherwise the land will vomit you out for defiling it, as it vomited out the nation that was before you."").

19. Buechner, *Wishful Thinking*, 80–81. That sadness may lead to joy, see further in the chapter "The Sowing of Tears."

"Do not prophesy," their prophets [the "false prophets"] say
"Do not prophesy about these things;
disgrace will not overtake us. (Mic 2:6)

Mic 2:6–11 is fraught with interpretive problems, but the most likely approach is that we are given ear to "dueling prophets." Eliezer of Beaugency (a medieval Jewish commentator) believes that Micah is countering the *false* prophets who charge that Micah is not a true prophet. Micah parries with a charge against their behavior:

But you rise up against my people as an enemy;
you strip the robe from the peaceful,
from those who pass by trustingly
with no thought of war.
The women of my people you drive out
from their pleasant houses;
from their young children you take away
my glory forever.

Jesus uses language very similar to Micah's when he says in Matt 7:15–20, "Beware of false prophets, who come to you in sheep's clothing but inwardly are ravenous wolves. You will know them by their fruits. Are grapes gathered from thorns, or figs from thistles? In the same way, every good tree bears good fruit, but the bad tree bears bad fruit. A good tree cannot bear bad fruit, nor can a bad tree bear good fruit. Every tree that does not bear good fruit is cut down and thrown into the fire. Thus you will know them by their fruits."

Micah calls their words "drivel": "If a person comes with spirit/wind of deceit [saying] I will *drivel* [prophesy] to you of wine and [spirited] drink, he would be a *driveling* prophet for this people" (Mic 2:11, my translation).

Micah exposes these idol-worshiping prophets as mere merchants. They deliver a favorable oracle if the people "feed" them: "Thus says the Lord concerning the prophets who lead my people astray, who cry 'Peace' when they have something to eat, but declare war against those who put nothing into their mouths" (Mic 2:4–5).

Micah follows this with a warning: "Therefore it shall be night to you, without vision, and darkness to you, without revelation. . . . The seers shall be disgraced, and the diviners put to shame; they shall all cover their lips, for there is no answer from God" (Mic 2:6–7) A prophet who neither sees nor speaks is not worth a farthing.

For the prophets of God false teaching naturally results in false actions. Beliefs have consequences, real and weighty. Micah is satirical in his mocking, for "who can refute a sneer?"[20]

That actions have consequences is clear to most of us. A corollary to that is that consequences also follow beliefs. That is less obvious, but the biblical authors show no doubt about it. Thus, if you believe in a god who "can't god," there is little that can follow by way of beneficial actions.

It is not simply that the gods of the nations are manufactured, but that the gods have no "substance." Jeremiah says it plain enough:

> Do not learn the way of the nations,
> or be dismayed at the signs of the heavens;
> for the nations are dismayed at them.
> For the customs of the peoples are false:
> a tree from the forest is cut down,
> and worked with an ax by the hands of an artisan;
> people deck it with silver and gold;
> they fasten it with hammer and nails
> so that it cannot move.
> Their idols are like scarecrows in a cucumber field,
> and they cannot speak;
> they have to be carried,
> for they cannot walk.
> Do not be afraid of them,
> for they cannot do evil,
> nor is it in them to do good. (Jer 10:2–5)

The word in v. 2, "customs," is the usual translation, but by what follows, Jeremiah clearly has "idols" in view. Jeremiah describes these idols as *hevel*, a word found often in wisdom texts. It is a favorite term of "the Preacher" (Ecclesiastes). The Preacher cuts through illusions, teaches an "earthed" humility (grounded in God as the consummate *giver*), encourages joys and pleasures, and yet knows the limits of worldly pleasures and the inevitability of death.[21]

A literal rendering of *hevel* would be something like "breath, vapor; vanity; foolish." In Ecclesiastes it often means "emptiness" or "meaningless." If the idols are *hevel*, as Jeremiah says, they are "unsubstantial"; they can't talk or walk; neither can they do ill—or good (Jer 7:3–5). Jeremiah contrasts the idols with the Lord, who is "true" (Jer 10:10, *'emet*; truth;

---

20. Reported to have been said by the eighteenth-century clergyman William Paley.

21. Cf. Davis, *Proverbs*, 159–63.

effectiveness; "massive substantiality" not "vapor"[22]). *The Message* renders it, "The real thing."

Jeremiah is drawing a vivid image for us here. "The imagination is the chief faculty of moral discernment," Ellen Davis reminds us.[23] The prophets certainly draw us to that truth with these images that surely not only shine but burn.

Jeremiah stretches our imagination beyond a narrowly literal, iconoclastic view of idols (though they are made of "bricks and mortar"). They are *hevel* at their core; lifeless, non-generative, and impotent.

What is at stake in idolatry is not simply the ludicrous nature of the mindset but the noxious behavior that ensues from such idolatry. Saint Paul admonishes the Roman church: "Claiming to be wise, they became fools; and they exchanged the glory of the immortal God for images resembling a mortal human being or birds or four-footed animals or reptiles. Therefore God gave them up in the lusts of their hearts to impurity, to the degrading of their bodies among themselves, because they exchanged the truth about God for a lie and worshiped and served the creature rather than the Creator, who is blessed forever! Amen" (Rom 1:22–25).

Hosea takes these consequences of idolatry beyond human behavior to include the effect it has for creation itself: "Therefore the land mourns, and all who live in it languish, together with the wild animals and the birds of the air, even the fish of the sea are perishing" (Hos 4:3).

Bad theology is tantamount not only to bad behavior but bad ecology as well. This point is graphically made by Micah as well:

Hear, you peoples, all of you;
listen, O earth, and all that is in it;
and let the Lord GOD be a witness against you,
the Lord from his holy temple.
For lo, the LORD is coming out of his place,
and will come down and tread upon the high places of the earth.
Then the mountains will melt under him
and the valleys will burst open,
like wax near the fire,
like waters poured down a steep place (Mic 1:2–4).

Idolatry not only affects humanity, it wreaks havoc on the landscape as well.

---

22. McKane, *Jeremiah*, 225.

23. Davis, *Proverbs*, 19.

To laugh at idols exposes their painted faces and costume jewelry; their idleness. It is the sheer incongruity of idolatry in the face of the living God that stokes the ire of the prophets, poets, and storytellers of Scripture. Fool's gold, indeed.

*

God takes no half affections.

—JOHN DONNE, QUOTED IN DAVIS, *PROVERBS*, 29

Ideology (as also tyranny, its sibling) is a generous foe for humor. But if, as C. S. Lewis says, the devil can't stand to be mocked, his minions, the idols, should be even more offended by the portrayal of idolatry in Scripture.

The idols, the logic of the accompanying worship, and the consequences of such worship are roundly ridiculed throughout Scripture. We have seen the idols de-divinized in several passages. However, even that doesn't seem sufficient for some authors. The idols are even dehumanized:

> They [the idols] have mouths, but do not speak;
> eyes, but do not see.
> They have ears, but do not hear;
> noses, but do not smell.
> They have hands, but do not feel;
> feet, but do not walk;
> they make no sound in their throats.
> Those who make them are like them;
> so are all who trust in them. (Ps 115:5–8)

There is nothing sacral or human about idols; being *formed* themselves, they are not part of God's "making." The formed gods are lifeless, powerless, useless. They have no working body parts: mouths with no speech, eyes that don't see, ears that are stone-deaf, noses that don't sniff, hands that are numb, immobile feet, and aphonic voices. As Davidson says, "Costly, well crafted they may be, but in the end of the day, they are but lifeless blocks of wood or metal, fit symbols of gods who can do nothing."[24]

If idols could be offended, assuredly they would be by the biblical portrayals of their craft.

---

24. Davidson, *Vitality*, 377.

Idols are anything we can't laugh at. This disposition is not obvious. The tenuous nature of so many of our beliefs and the strength of our favored foibles are best left alone, unquestioned. Don't even think about poking fun at these paramours of ours.

Idolatry reduced to a physical object is not a rich enough image to account for the various idolatries and ramifications in Scripture. Idolatry as a physical object is little more than the domestication of God, a talisman or fetish. More important to the authors of Scriptures is that the idol diverts living into the *Imago Dei* with all its entailments of holiness, fidelity, and truth. Idolatry is a failure to realize the uttermost otherness of God.

Idolatry may quell humor, but fuels laughter. If at first you don't succeed, make fun of it.

Bruising the Funny Bone

Humor, Charlie, usually needs a victim . . .

—ISABEL DALHOUSIE, IN McCALL SMITH'S
COMFORTS OF A MUDDY SATURDAY

A mocker is most himself amongst rogues and ne'er-do-wells. Fear-filled mollifiers pay him respect (but seldom respect him). Laughter, if it can be found at all with a mocker's comrades and victims, is as far from mirth as Nineveh is from Tarshish.

The Bible takes very seriously—and none too politely—those who scorn others: "Mocking a pauper—reviles his maker. Rejoicing over calamity—will not be cleared [from blame]" (Prov 17:5, my translation).

Reasons behind poverty and misfortune are not always transparent, however, and God takes it personally when those who suffer such adversities suffer further from fools who mock their misfortune. Poverty and wealth, fortune and misfortune are in God's domain and part of God's inscrutable will. Hannah, in her great prayer of praise for the gift of Samuel, her longed-for son, says, "The Lord makes poor and makes rich; he brings low, he also exalts" (1 Sam 2:7).

Our knowledge of fortune and misfortune, and our standards for judging such providences, are presumptuous. Such conceits show not only our arrogance but are an affront to God's character: "Do not boast about wearing fine clothes, and do not exalt yourself when you are honored; for the works of the Lord are wonderful, and his works are concealed from humankind" (Sir 11:4).

Mocking those who have suffered misfortune makes the would-be comic not a social critic but divine usurper.

The graphic portrayal of mocking in Prov 30:17 underscores the seriousness and aversion this action evokes: "An eye that mocks a father / and scorns obedience to a mother, / may the ravens of the valley peck it out, / and the young vultures eat it."

Apparently parents dealing with eye-rolling teenagers did not begin with baby-boomers listening to Elvis and The Beatles.

Those who have experienced mocking, scorn, and ridicule know them to be *cruel* jokes. The mockers are disdainful to the full extent they disdain.

> *"Scorners hold others in contempt and by doing so seal themselves off from the very wisdom they need to be brought to their senses." —Charry,* Happiness, *222*

★

Sociability without mockery and teasing and taunting would be both dreary and verging on the pointless.

—ADAM PHILLIPS, "'WHAT'S SO FUNNY?'" 128

In Addison's genealogy of false humor, Falsehood is the mother of Nonsense, who was "brought to bed of a son called Frenzy, who married one of the daughters of Folly commonly known by the name of Laughter, on whom he begot that monstrous infant of which I have been speaking."[1] The infant is Scorn. Even though this humor is false, it still comes under the umbrella of humor.

That leads to the question, "Is there any occasion when mockery and scorn may serve more noble causes than viciousness?" Adam Phillips makes such a suggestion that mocking may serve more "obliging purposes"; ridicule is part of our "sociability," he contends. Mockery may expose what we would otherwise not think of ourselves. Comedy "generously diminishes us; it lowers us down gently from our own ideals."[2] Mocking may serve our sociability and not just our sociopathologies in this view.

In Proverbs Lady Wisdom herself adopts scorn as one of her strategies for dealing with those who will not heed her counsel: "So I'll laugh at your disaster; / I'll scorn you when dread comes over you" (Prov 1:26; my translation).

1. Addison, *Essays*, 2.
2. Phillips, "What's So Funny?," 126.

This indictment by Lady Wisdom is similar to the prophetic indictments of judgment. Lady Wisdom raises her voice (Prov 1:20); her indictment may be a warning of sorts, though certainly one with potential dire consequences: "The time will come . . . but then it will be too late. . . ." Ellen Davis says that Wisdom tells the "simple ones" they must either "grow up or grow down in moral stature."[3] For now, however, if one chooses to ignore her, she will merely laugh at these gullible ones and then laugh the more so with what befalls them for ignoring her.

One role humor may play is that of *phronesis*, a practical reasoning; the art of moral judgment.

Despite the current concern for tolerance and banning "isms" of all sorts (racism, sexism, etc.), mockery, scorn, sarcasm, and the like are effective tools for countering the very things we say we disdain. Scorn runs with rogues, but scorn can also turn on the rogues with exacting force.

A fair question to ask of Lady Wisdom might be, "What are you attempting to achieve with your scorn?" Motivations are notoriously difficult and dangerous to ascertain. I often do things with the best of intentions that are not received as such. Still, at whom or at what is she laughing? Is Wisdom laughing because of the disaster that will ensue for the simpletons or at the triumph of right over error? Even though the road to hell is paved with good intentions, it does matter, doesn't it, whether she intends ill or something gentler with her scorn, such as correction? Discerning the character of the characters is important in humor as well as in moral judgments, though both are equally elusive. Even ne'er-do-wells *do well* occasionally.

Humor works with reversals. Lady Wisdom (and Scripture generally) delights in "reversal of fortune" circumstances. Lady Wisdom is not the

> *Proverbs has a rich vocabulary for Dunderheads. Michael Fox identifies these words and the words for various nuances of Wisdom in his Proverbs commentary. He says, "The essence of folly is lack of good judgment, with consequent distortions in moral and practical choices."[4] He notes that Proverbs uses six terms for Folly: "ignoramus"; "empty-headed"; being a "knave"; a "dolt"; "insolent"; and "gullible," with all the little nuances along the way.[5] There are nearly twice as many words for Wisdom.*

3. Davis, *Proverbs*, 33.

4. Fox, *Proverbs 1–9*, 38.

5. Fox, *Proverbs 1–9*, 39–43.

agent of disaster in our passage; she is the oracular force. She observes, she chides, warns, but does not intervene directly. Having disregarded her entreaty (Prov 1:24, "When I did call, you *spurned* me . . .") the consequence, should it come, is fitting, not her doing *per se*. There is something natural in reversals of fortune, though not deterministic. Her action may be more regulatory than disciplinary. Still, Lady Wisdom is not one with whom to trifle. What is said of the Comic Muse could be said of Lady Wisdom: "She is light and playful, but when ignored takes a most effective revenge."[6]

Perhaps, as Ellen Charry counsels, scorners and other manner of fools are "quite tiresome, and it is better to avoid them"; their "tragic flaw is that they cannot learn."[7] Yet Lady Wisdom herself employs scorn as a tactic that entreats us to learn from our experiences. For Lady Wisdom scorn begins with a simple observation about acts and consequences. Whether these acts and consequences are negative or positive, effective or not, mockery is part of human social interactions that get played out in the choices made.

> "There is the good mockery of everyday life that regulates our self-importance, and so relieves us of too much responsibility for the world. And there is the bad mockery that foists something upon us that we would rather, if we could choose, protect ourselves from." (Phillips, "What's So Funny?" 5)

Such behavior becomes an adjustment opportunity, often negatively, but not ineluctably so.

*

Der Mentsh trakht un Got lakht. [Man proposes; God laughs].

—YIDDISH PROVERB, QUOTED BY RUTH WISSE, *NO JOKE*, 184

The *virtuous* nature of scorn, if there be such a thing, comes mostly in passages outside Wisdom texts. A story that shows up twice in Scripture—an indication of its importance—is when Sennacherib comes against Jerusalem in the days of King Hezekiah (2 Kgs 18–19) and during the prophetic role of Isaiah (Isa 36–7). A letter is sent from the Assyrians

6. Buckley, *Morality*, 5.

7. Charry, *Happiness*, 222–23.

saying that Hezekiah should not be misled by his God, that the gods of the other nations could not stand against the Assyrians (and their gods), so why should Hezekiah think his God will stand?

Hezekiah prays to God, pointing out that Sennacherib has insulted the *living* God, not a "bricks and mortar" god of the other nations: "Incline your ear, O Lord, and hear; open your eyes, O Lord, and see; hear the words of Sennacherib, which he has sent to mock the living God. Truly, O Lord, the kings of Assyria have laid waste the nations and their lands, and have hurled their gods into the fire, though they were no gods but the work of human hands—wood and stone—and so they were destroyed" (2 Kgs 19:16–18).

God replies in words meant for Sennacherib's ears: "Whom have you mocked and reviled? Against whom have you raised your voice, and haughtily lifted your eyes? Against the Holy One of Israel!" (2 Kgs 19:22).

The scorn that God displays in this situation is scorn towards a prideful king. "Do you know about whom you're talking, Sennacherib?" In this brief passage God describes the actions of the Daughter of Zion who both despises and "tosses her head" towards the prideful monarch, a gesture of disdain towards him. The picture drawn is profligately cartoonish.

Scorn seems an appropriate riposte to the pride and contempt exhibited by Sennacherib. Scorn comes as a form of exposure, as Phillips notes, but also as *turnabout is fair play*, a standard inversion that delights humor. Sennacherib's scorn is misplaced and is exposed as a fault of judgment or of character, probably both, whereas the Daughter of Zion scorns the king's *hubris*. Sennacherib seeks to humiliate; God seeks to humble.

It could be said that God is acting disdainfully here, a *tit for tat* strategy on God's part. On the other hand, God is playing a similar role to Lady Wisdom with the fools in Proverbs. Maybe God is giving a direct—yet gentle—rebuke to counter the disdain of a haughty king. As with Lady Wisdom's scorn, however, there are dire consequences to be had should the king persist in his folly. In God's eyes, Sennacherib is more sovereign *usurper* than sovereign.

It seems easier to overlook scornful cheekiness than scornful *hubris*. Lady Wisdom chuckles at the fool, perhaps because a fool may still be led to some sense: "O ye simple ones, understand wisdom: and, ye fools, be ye of an understanding heart" (Prov 8:5). God excusing the prideful potentate for *hubris* is not so easily assuaged: "In the pride of his countenance the wicked does not seek him; all his thoughts are, "There is no God." (Ps 10:4). Yet, may scorning the scorner serve a *restorative* purpose? Can self-evaluation arise from being scorned?

"Thou [God] hast made us the reproach of our neighbors, the scorn and derision of those about us. . . . Rise up! Be a help for us! Ransom us for the sake of your faithfulness!" (Ps 44:13; 26).

That God could forego judgment occurs early on in the biblical narrative. When God comes down to see if Sodom and Gomorrah are as bad as everyone says, Abraham stands before the Lord and asks, "Will you really destroy the righteous with the wicked? . . . what if there were fifty righteous in the city, would you destroy and not uphold if there were fifty righteous in the place? . . . shall not the judge of all the earth act justly?" (Gen 18:23–25).

God concedes the point to Abraham that he would not act unjustly toward them if there were fifty righteous. Abraham, though, with hat in hand, continues to negotiate—haggles!—with God, getting God down to the "bargain price" that if there were ten righteous persons, God would not destroy the cities. Ellen Davis calls Abraham an "audacious intercessor" in this story.[8]

Apparently, though, they could not find even ten righteous men in the cities because God destroyed them. Lot tried to warn his family, telling them to get out of the city for the Lord was about to destroy the city. His sons-in-law, however, thought he was jesting (Gen 19:14). "She [Comic Muse] is light and playful, but when ignored takes a most effective revenge."[9]

The scorned righteous can appeal to God for help. Having their own folly exposed by scorn, the righteous, in a turnabout move, admonishes, through scorn, those who persist in folly. "The righteous will see and fear, and will laugh at him [the evildoer], saying, 'Behold the one who would not put strength in God'" (Ps 52:6–7a).

Is there a righteous scorn for the scorned righteous?

---

8. Davis, *Prophecy*, 25.

9. Buckley, *Morality*, 5.

God is rightly portrayed as "laughing" sinners "to scorn";
his "laughter" teaches a salutary lesson.

—M. A. SCREECH, *LAUGHTER AT THE FOOT OF THE CROSS*, 42

Can God simply *laugh scorn off*—not only for the victim but the per-petrator? "The One who sits in the heavens laughs," the psalmist tells us, even though the nations conspire against the Lord's people (Ps 2:4a).

Ps 2 stands out as problematic for contemporary sensibilities concern-ing scorn. Having been lacerated by scorn, we have learned to hold scorn in contempt. We *scorn* scorn. Is Ps 2 an odd case where "two wrongs" actu-ally does make a right? Is a *righteous* scorn to be had? Lady Wisdom dem-onstrates this possibility when she employs scorn as a defensive measure (Prov 1:26).

Sennacherib is not named in Ps 2, but the psalm smacks of his de-meanor. Haughty is an apt term to describe the stance of this monarch.

Chutzpah: *Tvzi Freeman writing for Chabad.org says that* chutzpah *can be good or bad, but whichever, it is always extreme—"destructive and ugly or vital and fantas-tic" but never in between, he says. Often cited in this respect is the* Mishnah *where we are entreated to be "fierce as a leopard." Freeman says that Abraham had* chutzpah *to argue with God over Sodom and Gomorrah. That's "good"* chutzpah. *Sennacherib, I would argue, is* chutzpah *at its worst.*

Chutzpah might come into play. In Ps 2 God deals with the scorning nations who conspire against God's anointed by scorning the scorners. This response on God's part casts further light on scorn and humor's *moral* role in our lives. Ps 2:4 reads: "He who sits in the heavens laughs; the Lord has them in derision."

This is the same word pair for "laugh" and "scorn/make fun of" that is used of Lady Wisdom's actions in Prov 1:26. These two passages invite further reflection regarding scorn.

It is not uncommon to pass the words of Ps 2:4 off as an anthropo-morphism. Humans may laugh; God decidedly doesn't.[10] Even if it were sim-ply anthropomorphism, what do these

---

10. Alfred North Whitehead is reported to have said, "The total absence of humor from the Bible is one of the most singular things in all literature."

words of scorn by God achieve for us as they stand? What does the image convey about scorn, the Deity, and humanity?

The overbearing arrogance of potentates—Sennacherib is *exemplar par excellence*—is exposed as misguided, at best. The one who considers his power limitless is shown powerless by the One who sits in the heavens. The rulers reach for the heavens—and discover laughter, scornful laughter. They *founder* in laughter. The ridiculing victimizer becomes the victim ridiculed. Yet is there ever hope for the scorner?

In Proverbs we may detect a certain *playfulness* with the words Lady Wisdom speaks. She gives a stern warning, but one where a wink and a firm look may suffice for correction. With God in Ps 2, there appears no sign of playfulness, even though we could render Ps 2:4 as "The one who sits in the heavens is *amused*; the Lord laughs at them."[11]

However, the laughter of God is followed by a sobering statement, rendered aptly by the Coverdale translation of the Bible: "Then he shall speak unto them in his wrath; and vex them in his sore displeasure."

Something at first frightful may turn amusing if the fright is benign. That's a big "if" here. There is clearly a victim in God's merriment and a warning, much more so than with Lady Wisdom in Proverbs. God is *vexed* in his displeasure, as Coverdale makes clear. After Lady Wisdom mocks the simpletons, she says, "But those who listen to me will be secure and will live at ease, without dread of disaster" (Prov 1:33). There is no telling smile that she is amused but there is an opening, should the fools heed her advice. Could the same be true of God's laughter at the prideful kings who conspire against the people of God?

*

To be mocked, in other words, is the narcissist's nightmare.

—ADAM PHILLIPS, "'WHAT'S SO FUNNY?'" 126

Calling the kings of Ps 2 "victims" needs qualification. They are certainly not *hapless* victims, as may be true in some sense of the simple or gullible ones in Proverbs. Scorn—even anger—is appropriate for those who have no regard for others. That kings, like Sennacherib, show no regard

---

11. Goldingay, *Psalms I*, 99 (emphasis added). Goldingay further comments, "God's reaction is *merriment and scorn*: the second verb makes clear that there is a *serious side* to Yhwh's smile. . . . Yhwh does not take them with the seriousness with which they take themselves."

for the *living, covenantal* God of Israel and instill terror upon the Lord's anointed, calls for some response. The rulers of Ps 2, the scornful children of Proverbs who overreach themselves, and others of a haughty nature standing to lose even what they did have for the sake of what they thought they could obtain, has at least of modicum of "justice" about it. *Lex comicae,* if not actually *lex talionis.*

A more interesting question—and a harder one—is whether there can be an adjustment opportunity, beyond the crippling hand that mockery often yields.

Mocking the mockers exposes the fatal flaws of their misplaced, short-lived laughter. Ps 2 attests that tyrants should indeed fear funniness.

The Lord's scorn, and the warning laughter of Lady Wisdom, unmasks arrogance, pride, and haughtiness. I doubt that Sennacherib and his kind would find humor in this unmasking. I'm equally sure that the ancient Israelites just might.

Mocking, ridicule, and the like can expose flaws, but there is a qualification for that observation: "For mockery to work, something about a person has to be exposed, usually something they would prefer to conceal from themselves and others because it is at odds with the person they would rather be. And what is exposed has to be described in such a way as to render it amusing."[12]

In the movie Life Is Beautiful, *set amidst the occupation and cruelty of the Nazis, the antics of Guido, the main character, give his son something to laugh about. In a particularly touching scene, the son, Joshua, sees Guido taken away by a Nazi soldier. As Guido leaves, he marches in "goose-step" like Nazis would. He looks back at his son with a smile and gives him a wink; the son winks back with a smile. It is a hopeful gesture in an otherwise hopeless and brutal situation. Tyrants fear funniness.*

The mockery and laughter of Guido in the movie Life Is Beautiful *dispels fear by exposing the automatous nature of the perpetrators. Much the same is true of Lady Wisdom's laughter that exposes the imprudence of the young fools. Phillips says that when "we laugh at someone else, we violate, or simply disregard, their preferred image of themselves. To be mocked, in other words, is the narcissist's nightmare."[13]*

With the actions of Guido in Life Is Beautiful *we are in a different realm of moral education from the cruelty that the king in Ps 2 exhibits, one that shows a more benevolent bent than mere cruelty.*

12. Phillips, "What's So Funny?," 128 (emphasis added).
13. Phillips, "What's So Funny?," 126; Benigni, *Life Is Beautiful.*

The laughter of Sennacherib's scorn is far from amusing. I'm inclined to view such laughter as a *counterfeit* of laughter, void of either amusement or moral education. Whatever amusement achieved is short-lived because what Sennacherib and his ilk expose is fear. The moral value of this sort of laughter improves nothing for either victim or victimizer. The mortal mockers in Ps 2 framed their mocking void of any sympathy or corrective intent other than total submission. The words of another set of scorners show mockery clearly and maliciously: "Let's see how God handles this one; since God likes him so much, let *Him* help him!" (Ps 22:8, *The Message*).

This attitude of the scorners in Ps 2 leaves no room for the scorned to reconsider or try to rectify the situation (other than capitulation). In contrast, Lady Wisdom leaves a door open with her scorn: "I'll laugh for now, *but. . .*" The same may be true for Ps 2 by God, though not expressly stated. Lady Wisdom and God *test* persons with mocking laughter, and if the test is unheeded, further action may be necessary.

*

Laughter must purge before it can redeem.

—TERRY LINDVALL, *GOD MOCKS*, 5

Most commentators do not linger over God's mocking laughter in Ps 2. A notable exception is Martin Luther. Luther sees these words as "consoling" for "we" in the church might feel "faintheartedness" by the "multitude and magnitude of the world's majesties."[14]

It is not out of contempt that God opposes the adversaries of the church, Luther claims, though certainly out of disapproval. We should note that we are not told explicitly what causes the Lord to laugh; it can be inferred that the rulers who come against the people of God are overestimating their power and underestimating God's investment in these people. Luther gives this scenario: "Children present an amusing spectacle when they try to slay dogs or swine with blades of straw, as if with a knife. Nor can any one of us restrain his laughter if he sees a fool take a twig in his hands, run with great exertion against a tower, and so try to overthrow it. For such an attempt would be foolish and vain."[15]

14. Luther, *Selected Psalms*, 22.

15. Luther, *Selected Psalms*, 22–23.

Luther, though, is also not unsparing in his own contempt of these rulers, calling them "miserable reptiles."[16] Luther is quick to say, however, that this is a "new and unheard voice" that God would laugh at the adversaries and not simply dispense with them. He says that "reason" might suspect that if God does nothing against these adversaries that either God does not see this egregious behavior on the part of the rulers, or that God is weak because God doesn't suppress such evil persons. "Reason" might suspect that God is either "stupid" or "wicked."[17] The Holy Spirit, though, shows us that these "blasphemies" will not go on unheeded. "We" find consolation because God does see and is not silent. God laughs.

Luther proceeds with these thoughts and observes that this passage shows God "not so swiftly moved to anger as we." He says, "[God] laughs a while, not only because He sees that such attempts are vain, but because he grants *time for repentance.*"[18]

Luther sees these words as a great consolation for those who suffer at the hands of the powers and the powerful, those that cause "uproars, rage, and take counsel together"; these men are "shameful . . . cruel . . . odious." When "we" understand that God laughs at them, we also shall laugh [as Guido laughs in *Life Is Beautiful*] and not grow angry. "[The powerful] provide God with jests and jokes, present a carnival play for him, when they are at their angriest. And when they are preoccupied with such thoughts and undertakings, they are most assuredly nothing else than a joke factory, or, as we say in German, 'Our Lord God's bag of tricks.'"[19]

> Weiser likens God's actions in Ps 2 to, "A race of pigmies face to face with a giant," (Weiser, Psalms, 112).

Viewed in this way, mockery forms a more recognizable form of moral education. As victims mocked by the power persons, we should "fortify our hearts" against these assaults and see them for what they are—vain attempts against the power of heaven. Furthermore, we may take solace in this image of the laughter of God at the injustice and impiety of these people. God's

16. Luther's diatribe over several pages in his commentary on this issue includes, but is not limited to: Turks, popes, kings, demons, Satan, furious men, Anabaptists, Sacramentarians, peace-disturbers, sectarians, tyrants, impious men, bishops, sin, and even our own conscience, our "greatest enemy." I think Luther may be giving reptiles a bad name by lumping them with the rest on his list.

17. Luther seems to be responding here to some readers of Ps 2.

18. Luther, *Selected Psalms*, 23 (emphasis added).

19. Luther, *Selected Psalms*, 25.

mockery is a weapon against their injustices, horrors, and so forth. Taking solace in God's justice is a moral education that can produce courage and patience.

Luther's approach lines up rather nicely with Wells's improvisational approach. Over-accept the offer by incorporating it into a larger framework of God's work in the world.

This is trickier. Luther launches into a long discussion on God's patience in the face of various evils by tyrants of all kinds, secular and spiritual. And, though God often seems intolerably patient in these matters to us, Luther assures his audience that the leaders will be exposed for their folly.[20]

This patience of God would be in accord with Lady Wisdom's mockery at the simple ones in Proverbs. Mockery from this perspective could serve *restorative* measures then, even for those who otherwise fall into the snare of *hubris*.

Luther is clear that this patience of God is not unconditional (as v. 5 indicates): "For even if He who dwells in the heavens laughs for a time at the vain attempts of the godless, nevertheless He will not laugh forever."[21] Luther is blunt that God's wrath is as real as his laugh. "For, when the Lord is angry, it is no play, no joke."[22] Luther continues, saying that the godless will feel God's word of anger "if they do not turn and come to repentance."[23] Erasmus echoes this sentiment when he says that God's laughter in Ps 2 is "a metaphor but not an empty one."[24]

For Luther Ps 2:4 is more for the consolation of those who are now oppressed and fearful of those who wield power mercilessly and defy God. God's mocking laughter in this situation is comforting, but also shows God's patience, something that Luther returns to mostly for our benefit, but by extension it could also be seen for the benefit of the powerful, should they see their folly. Laughter is a forerunner to warn of God's impending wrath; mocking may alert us to more dire consequences should we persist in our folly.

For Luther laughter is a spiritual tool as well as a practical one. It's a practical tool in that "howling and complaining" gain us nothing. As a spiritual tool we must learn to laugh, as God laughs, at the folly of the scorners. However, we must also learn that these things that terrify us and

---

20. Luther, *Selected Psalms*, 22–35.

21. Luther, *Selected Psalms*, 29.

22. Luther, *Selected Psalms*, 32.

23. Luther, *Selected Psalms*, 32.

24. Screech, *Laughter*, 44.

"accuse" us—even our own impiety, foolishness, profanity, blasphemy, turbulence, and unquietness—are also to be laughed at since they are equally "comical spectacles." For Luther Christ's forgiveness is the "highest article of faith." When we learn to laugh at assaults by our scornful enemies we will each become "a true doctor of theology."[25]

*

The *drye mock*. Not sarcasm, which is like vinegar, or cynicism, which is so often the voice of disappointed idealism, but a delicate casting of a cool and illuminating light on life, and thus an enlargement."

—ROBERTSON DAVIES, *THE CUNNING MAN*, 150

Mockery, ridicule, sarcasm, and the like, while often and usually vices, can also be virtues when used to counter injustices, abuses of power, misplaced pride, and so forth. These tools of humor, then, can serve as moral educa-tion (which is usually lost on those who need it most).[26] Mocking may give heart to those who are fainthearted at the hands of the powerful or give a renewed heart to one who falls prey to pride and arrogance. Mockery as a tool rather than a weapon may serve as an improvisational tactic, inviting an adjustment opportunity.

Luther's approach, if I read it correctly, reminds me somewhat of the scene in *Prince Caspian* by C. S. Lewis where Aslan (the lion) confronts Trumpkin (the dwarf) who doesn't believe in lions. "Come here," Aslan roars. Trumpkin is justifiably terrified by this encounter. Aslan, though, picks him up as a mother lion would pick up her cub and tosses him into the air, only to gently catch him. "'Son of Earth, shall we be friends?' asked Aslan. 'Ye--he--he--hes,' panted the Dwarf."[27]

> "With sovereign contempt [God] surveys these petty plotting, and when the moment comes confounds them with a word."
> —Kirkpatrick, Psalms, 9

I'm hard-pressed to see the mocking either of Sennacherib or God as a *joke*

---

25. Luther, *Selected Psalms*, 28.

26. Fables and other storytelling strategies also serve as moral instruction that forgoes a blunt approach.

27. Lewis, *Prince Caspian*, 148–49.

proper in Ps 2, but we might see this as an instance of *drye mock*. The rulers, supposing a position of invincibility, take a stand and hold a conclave to do evil. All the while God sits above them, ready—and able!—to forestall any actions against God's "anointed [ones]." The "caption" would read: *Der Mentsh trakht un Got lakht*: People strive and God snickers.

Drye mock opens new possibilities for consideration of this justifiably maligned trope: Can a point of personal moral educational be realized by both mocked and mocker? The role of *phronesis*, a discerning and humble heart, may guide the use and understanding of mocking humor in daily endeavors.

I can't help but wonder that if the rulers came to their senses and caught the force of the scorn and forewent their tyranny that the Lord would, like Aslan, find a way to "catch" them in his hands as well.

A Shepherd Gets Caught by a Sheep

(Vignette)

To have a positive outcome with humor generally requires an intimacy of sorts between the participants. When Sennacherib laughs from his perch at the Israelites huddled behind their walls, the laughter is pernicious. Sennacherib is not inviting anything but subjection. Change is not invited but imposed. This is not an adjustment opportunity from Sennacherib.

Not so with the biblical prophets.

After a series of military and political victories, King David, the beloved of the Lord, the shepherd of his people, makes a "fateful and fatal error."[1] Fox observes that the Bible seldom settles for whitewashed heroes— and it does so with a "considerable amount of artistic skill."[2]

King David decides not to go out to battle, as kings were expected to do "in the spring" (2 Sam 11). David stays back, enjoying the fruits of his previous battles that ensured his kingship. Then, one afternoon, in the cool of the day, while lounging on the veranda, David spots Bathsheba bathing. He invites her to his house. Was it entrapment? Collusion? Or garden variety "I did it my way . . ." mentality?

Not long after, the prophet Nathan comes to David complaining of a gross injustice occurring within David's kingdom. A rather wealthy person has absconded a sheep from his dirt-poor neighbor to feed a stranger who had come into their village. David knows full well the sheep–shepherd

---

1. Fox, *Early Prophets*, 470. The "error," as Fox goes on to say, is David behaving "as kings throughout the ages have done, taking what is not his and overstepping the bounds of both private morality and Israel's covenant with God."

2. Fox, *Early Prophets*, 470.

relationship. This is wrong, plain and simple. David, with all of his kingly voice, says, "Show me this SOD [Sire of a Dunderpate]!"[3]

The prophet, as we soon realize, is not presenting a court case, something David the king would know full well how to handle. Rather, the prophet offers King David a *mashal*, a parable. Nathan is holding the powerful King David to a higher power. The kingdom of God and the kingdoms of this world are never the same.

Nathan's parable is not a funny ha-ha moment, but it does draw David into an adjustment opportunity. Indeed, David gets caught by his own words and judgment. It is a classic *gotcha* joke: "Oh, look, you have a spot on your shirt . . ."—and then a tweak at the nose when the unsuspecting person looks down. It is a clever move by Nathan the prophet, one based on knowing the king–prophet relationship and the God–king relationship.

*

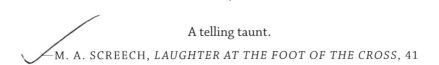

A telling taunt.

—M. A. SCREECH, *LAUGHTER AT THE FOOT OF THE CROSS*, 41

The beloved Micah, speaking over a century later, similarly directs care-filled words to friends in his neighborhood, those in the Shephelah region of Judah. The lowlands are the easiest pathway for an invading army to come against the people of God; in the days of the prophet Micah these villages were ravaged by such an army. Micah speaks a lament over his neighbors, not a parable, as Nathan does (cf. Mic 1:10–16).

The effect of this lament, however, is similar to that of Nathan's parable in that Micah invites his neighbors to return to the Lord's way, to have an adjustment opportunity. In Micah's case, the lament plays off the town names surrounding that region. David was caught by his own words whereas the towns are caught by their own *names*. Micah parodies their names in his dirge over the devastation that occurred by this invading foe.

Micah employs a lament form that would be well-known to his audience, being modeled on the lament David spoke over the death of his dear friend, Jonathan, and King Saul (2 Sam 1). Micah begins with David's own words, "Tell it not in Gath . . ." (cf. 2 Sam 1:20). The Hebrew words "tell" and

---

3. Cf. 2 Sam 12:5–6, "As the Lord lives, the man who has done this deserves to die; he shall restore the lamb fourfold, because he did this thing, and because he had no pity."

"Gath" sound similar. More importantly, Micah is specifically drawing his audience into the lament by using these very familiar words.

Micah's lament, however, takes a turn from the original lament. David laments, "Tell it not in Gath . . . lest the daughters of the Philistines rejoice" (1 Sam 1:20). Micah echoes the first couple of words from David's lament, but then breaks with the 1 Samuel text by saying, "Do not even wail": "In Gath, do not announce [your grief]; don't even weep" (Mic 1:10a). This lament expresses grief, but it is a grief they have brought upon themselves, through their disregard of God's teachings: "All this is for the transgression of Jacob / and for the sins of the house of Israel" (Mic 1:5a). Micah continues this parody of the David lament,[4] not by extolling fallen heroes but by *announcing* various consequences that ensue based on the names of the fallen towns.

Micah engages his audience through these wordplays on the various town names. For example, the people in Beth-Leaphrah (House of Dust/Dustville) are to "roll themselves/wallow [in the dust]" (Mic 1:10b); the "beautiful one" (Shaphir) is told to "[go out] in naked-shame" (Mic 1:11a); "Exit-Town" (Zaanan) is not to "flee" (Mic 1:11b). Micah creates puns for various towns in the region: your names portend your consequences!

Micah ends this lament with "unto Adullam, glory will come" (Mic 1:15b), perhaps a nod to the end of David's life when he fled to Adullam and where David is once again portrayed as a "selfless military leader" (2 Sam 23).[5] If so, this rounds out the poem with a word of hope in an otherwise dispiriting lament.

Micah's words sound harsh rather than comforting. But surrounding these harsh words are two things that mitigate seeing them as a blanket indictment. As an introduction to this lament, Micah shows his kinship with the people by speaking in the first person: "For this *I will lament* and wail / *I will go barefoot and naked* / I will make lamentation like the jackals / and mourning like the ostriches" (Mic 1:8). Micah stands with the people in their lament, just as David stands with the people of God lamenting the fallen king.[6]

---

4. Parodies can be sympathetic or satirical; parodies employ similar words and are imitative of a form. Parodies either lampoon their source or pay homage. Here Micah pays homage to David's original lament.

5. See, e.g., Fox, *Early Prophets*, 536.

6. For more details on Mic 1:10–15, see Petrotta, *Lexis Ludens*, 65–85.

Not only does Micah show himself as companion with the people, but
God also shows a willingness to be interrogated:

> "O my people, what have I done to you?
>   In what have I wearied you? Answer me!
> For I brought you up from the land of Egypt
>   and redeemed you from the house of slavery . . .
> O my people, remember now what King Balak of Moab devised
>   what Balaam son of Beor answered him
> and what happened from Shittim to Gilgal
>   that you may know the saving acts of the Lord" (Mic 6:3–5).

Micah and the Lord are neither insensitive nor impartial to the plight
of God's people. Rather, Micah shepherds his flock by sharing their lament.
There is an intimacy to Micah's words even as they point out a truth the
people would rather not hear. And God—known as a shepherd in Scripture
(Ps 23:1)—searches God's own heart. God inverts his role as judge and puts
himself on trial (Mic 6:3–4) to see if somehow God bears fault in their going from God. God also reminds them of a core story where God protected
the people, even from enemies they didn't know were plotting against them,
Balak and Balaam.

*

He frequently stepped on toes, never on feelings.

—GUY DAVENPORT, *EVERY FORCE EVOLVES A FORM*, 66

Similar to Micah's parody of David's lament, there is a strong possibility that in two instances Jesus parodies a familiar passage from Ezekiel
where shepherding imagery is used to criticize the behavior of the leaders
of Israel. In Ezekiel 34, the leaders of Israel are portrayed as shepherds who
cannot be bothered to feed the flock, or care for injured sheep, or search for
scattered sheep. Instead, they plunder and slaughter the flock for their own
personal benefit. God's response is a promise to remove those leaders and
shepherd his flock personally (Ezek 34:1–31).

Jesus draws upon these familiar images from Ezekiel to criticize the
Pharisees and other religious leaders of his day. In John 10:12, Jesus gives
a cartoonish image of a hired hand fleeing from a wolf rather than standing his ground and fighting for his sheep. This would have evoked in his

audience not only a smile, but also a memory of the Ezekiel shepherds caring only for themselves. Jesus goes on to describe himself as a shepherd similar to God's self-description in Ezekiel: he shepherds his flock personally and gives himself sacrificially for the sheep. "I am the good shepherd. The good shepherd lays down his life for the sheep. . . . I am the good shepherd. I know my own and my own know me" (John 10:11–15).

The imagery of Ezekiel 34 is also evident in Luke 15, where tax collectors and sinners come to hear the words of Jesus and where the Pharisees and scribes grumble that Jesus keeps company with sinners (Luke 15:1). Jesus speaks of a shepherd who notices that one sheep in a flock of one hundred sheep is missing. He asks of his audience, "Which one of you, having a hundred sheep and losing one of them, does not leave the ninety-nine in the wilderness and go after the one that is lost until he finds it?" (15:4). When the shepherd finds the lost sheep, he places it on his shoulders, comes back, and tells his friends and neighbors, "Rejoice with me, for I have found my sheep that was lost" (15:6). The outlandish extravagance of the shepherd's care parallels that of God in Ezekiel 34.

The parable about the sheep always struck me as a bad business model. A friend who went to Wharton Business School, tells me that if the effort is more than the value, you shouldn't do it. Jesus is not a good businessman. The life of faith is not about business, but about intimacy and grace.

Biblical stories seldom sermonize. They give a scene and enough details to warrant a sapient reading. Nathan and Micah, Jesus and even God, stand alongside the people rather than simply scolding them. There seems to be a trust based upon shared values and shared goals, a truthful following of God through all the vagaries of life. Humor works best with such intimacy.

Intimacy is crucial when the humor is most pointed. Nathan gets away with his subterfuge only because there is a trust between the prophet and the king. Micah is a neighbor, a countryman, to the people in that region, and probably suffered much as they did. Jesus, the shepherd, gives all of himself to gather all that is lost.

In each of these cases the point is made—and no blood is shed. Humor, if funny, seeks to woo more than command.

Whoa, Jesus!

A critic once remonstrated with me saying, with an air of indignant
reasonableness, "If you must make jokes, at least you need not make
them on such serious subjects."

—G. K. CHESTERTON, "ON MR. MCCABE
AND A DIVINE FRIVOLITY," 157

What could less conventional than a nonagenarian barren woman bearing a child? Let's see . . . How about a virgin having a baby? Whoa!

God seldom does the same thing twice, but God does love improvising on certain themes. God has a penchant towards the "little, the least, and the lost." It starts with Adam and Eve. They have tremendous freedom—and one little *thou shalt not*: "You may freely eat of every tree of the garden; but of the tree of the knowledge of good and evil you shall not eat" (Gen 2:16b–17a). They, of course, eat from the forbidden tree.

After that little misstep, God chooses Abraham and Sarah to be a blessing for the rest of us (Gen 12:1–3). We are told, however, that "Sarah was barren; she had no child" (Gen 11:30). Sarah is not a fertile "hen." If that is not bad enough, we are told that Abraham is seventy-five years old (Gen 12:4). Abraham is an aging rooster.

Maybe God likes playing from behind more than being the favored team all the time. Then again, if God only stacks the deck (to mix images), then we would complain that it is unfair. God can't win. Better, maybe, designating winners and losers is the wrong stategy in God's universe.

A little less than two millennia after a ninety-year-old barren woman bears a child, God does something equally surprising, and functionally the

123

polar opposite. The angel Gabriel comes to Mary saying, "Greetings, favored one! The Lord is with you" (Luke 1:28). Ten verses later, Mary (unlike Sarah) readily embraces the angel's word, "Here am I, the servant of the Lord; let it be with me according to your word" (Luke 1:38).

"How odd of God to choose the Jews." (Usually attributed to William Norman Ewer, d. 1976. Of course, there must be a rejoinder to such a statement: "Not odd of God / Goyim annoy 'im" ["goy" is the Hebrew word for Gentile].)

Douglas Adams developed an annotated script for the genealogy of Jesus, *The Prostitute in the Family Tree*.[1] There are responses to the various names, cheers and boos predominate the genealogy, but along the way are a few "huh?" responses ("Herzon the father of Aram"). There is also Rahab, who is designated a prostitute (boo), but when noted that she saved God's people, we hear cheers. Ruth, the faithful foreigner, also gets cheers. Adams makes this point: "We experience the humor when we see the whole story, but we miss the humor when the text is taken out of context."[2]

When we open our ears to the echoes and contrasts that run through and between the stories, we begin to see a pattern of God doing non-God-like things, like using individuals of questionable character to play central roles in delivering his people: Rahab the harlot (Josh 2, 6) and Ruth, a widow, an orphan, and a sojourner.[3] God is not inherently a respecter of persons. All are welcome at the banquet feast (see, e.g., Luke 14:13).

Jesus uses the mustard seed—the smallest of seeds—to image the kingdom of God. Jesus explains that a mustard seed "is the smallest of all the seeds on earth; yet when it is sown it grows up and becomes the greatest of all shrubs, and puts forth large branches, so that the birds of the air can make nests in its shade" (Mark 4:30–32). Joel Marcus makes this observation: "*Already* it [the Markan community of faith] finds that its weakness becomes the arena in which God's strength is displayed, that its suffering becomes the occasion of joy."[4]

Humor woos us into cultivating a life where convention is held lightly.

---

1. Adams, *Prostitute*, 4–5.

2. Adams, *Prostitute*, 5.

3. Davis, *Opening*, 167.

4. Marcus, *Mark 8–16*, 330.

✦

> Under the aspects of sex and death it is difficult to take social
> ambitions very seriously.
>
> —PETER BERGER,
> "CHRISTIAN FAITH AND SOCIAL COMEDY," 125

The picture of Jesus meek and mild is not one that holds up to scrutiny. Herod, various disciples (especially Peter), and the poor woman at the well simply coming to draw water come under Jesus' watchful eye. It is for the scrupulously religious ones, however, that Jesus saves his most barbed remarks: "Woe unto you, scribes and Pharisees, hypocrites!" (Matt 23:13).

Jesus goes on to call them not only hypocrites—one of his favorite terms—but also blind guides, fools, whitewashed tombs, serpents, and vipers as well (Matt 23:13, 16, 17, 27). Jesus uses these harsh terms in the context of their employing God's *Torah* for arguably self-serving ends. Jesus exposes the discrepancy between intentions, actions, and outcomes. As Berger notes, it is a discrepancy between spirit and world more so than life and matter.[5] It matters deeply, apparently, since Jesus begins with "hypocrites" (Matt 23:13) and ends with "vipers" (Matt 23:33) and even "murderers" (Matt 23:35).

These leaders in Jesus' day "bind heavy burdens and grievous to be borne and lay them on men's shoulders; but they themselves will not move them with one of their fingers"(Matt 23:4, KJV). In the face of the social drama of Jesus' day, the burdens foisted on the average citizen are undermined by the humorous images Jesus employs to characterize the actions of the religiously elite. Jesus is a consummate cartoonist in this diatribe against these leaders.

John Chrysostom, writing over three centuries later, laments that not much had changed in the practices and deeds of church leaders: "It brings me to tears even now when I hear mention of the best seats and salutations, and when I hear of the great troubles that have arisen from this for the churches of God" (Williams, Matthew, 435).

Gundry introduces this section of Matthew by noting, "These leaders stand not only for Jewish officials who were persecuting the church at

---

5. Berger, "Social Comedy," 124.

the time of Matthew's writing, but also, it appears, for antinomian eccle-siastics—'loophole lawyers' coming from the Pharisaical sect—who were exercising great influence in the church."[6]

Berger observes that humanity "exists as a conscious being in an un-conscionable world" and goes on to say, "It is in this basically human dis-crepancy that the clue to the comic is to be sought."[7] Jesus seems to concur in Matt 23 for he creates a series of images that expose the "unconscio-nableness" of the actions of some leaders towards those whom they are to serve and lead.

Jesus likely learned his craft through the words of his prophetic fore-bears. Micah says of the leaders of his own day, "Concerning evil, with both hands they do it!" (Mic 2:1). The leaders are ambidextrous in doing evil. Those who devise evil against God's people will find out that turnabout is fair play as God devises evil against them (Mic 2:2–3). Tit for tat is not the usual image for justice in Scripture, but for humor it works quite well.[8]

We see a similar pattern of contrasting images in Jesus' words to the scribes and Pharisees, rendered by Peterson as: "You're hopeless, you reli-gion scholars and Pharisees! Frauds! You keep meticulous account books, tithing on every nickel and dime you get, but on the meat of God's Law, things like fairness and compassion and commitment—the absolute ba-sics!—you carelessly take it or leave it. Careful bookkeeping is commend-able, but the basics are required. Do you have any idea how silly you look, writing a life story that's wrong from start to finish, nitpicking over commas and semicolons?" (Matt 23:23–24, *The Message*).[9]

What captures our attention in this rendering of the "gnat" and "camel" image that Jesus originally employed is the concern over a technical gram-matical issue while losing sight of the story as a whole. Peterson captures the force of what Jesus is imaging for his audience with this literary image.

6. Gundry, *Matthew*, 453.

7. Berger, "Social Comedy," 124.

8. In Ps 2 God "devises" evil against those who devise evil against the people of God; see the "Bruising the Funny Bone" chapter.

9. Peterson, in this rendering, takes the "gnat" and "camel" images and renders them with a writing image, a nice way to allow contemporary readers to hear afresh these words. Gundry, *Matthew*, 464, makes the point on the original rendering that a gnat is the smallest animal and a camel is the largest animal they would likely see in daily life. There is also a wordplay in the Aramaic between these two animals. Finally, these two animals would be forbidden based on the dietary laws.

Torah (what we often render as "law") is part of a *story* of God with God's people, not primarily a principle of jurisprudence.[10]

Jesus carries this tactic of contrasting images forward in the following verses as well: "Woe to you, scribes and Pharisees, hypocrites! For you clean the outside of the cup and of the plate, but inside they are full of greed and self-indulgence. You blind Pharisee! First clean the inside of the cup, so that the outside also may become clean. Woe to you, scribes and Pharisees, hypocrites! For you are like whitewashed tombs, which on the outside look beautiful, but inside they are full of the bones of the dead and of all kinds of filth. So you also on the outside look righteous to others, but inside you are full of hypocrisy and lawlessness" (Matt 23:25–28).

Jesus is not using the cup and plate images in terms of ritual purity but rather connects the clean/unclean distinction with hypocrisy and indulgence, suggesting a more metaphorical interpretation, indicating "disobedience to God's moral law."[11] Similarly, the tomb image suggests lack of inward purity, not directly ritual purity. Jesus makes the "ritual practice figurative of an ethical point."[12]

Jesus uses common, contrasting images to show the inconsistency between belief and practice. The upshot of these observations by Jesus reflects a form of practical reasoning that is associated with what we have come to call the virtues. These virtues rely upon imitative practices, listening to, watching, and adopting practices of others—Moses, Micah, Jesus, and those who came after them but who display wisdom gained from scripture, tradition and reason.

Prophets are not always easy people to be around. T. W. Manson said this of Jesus: "Some of the most tragic utterances of our Lord are evoked by the refusal of the Jewish people to recognize and accept him and the good things he offered."[13] Manson then cites

> "Reflecting on the quality of one's life before God is a taste to be cultivated." —Charry, Renewing, 19

Matt 23:37: "Jerusalem, Jerusalem, the city that kills the prophets and stones those who are sent to it! How often have I desired to gather your children together as a hen gathers her brood under her wings, and you

---

10. See also the "Irrevocable Decrees" Vignette.

11. Gundry, *Matthew*, 465.

12. Gundry, *Matthew*, 466.

13. Manson, *Servant*, 60.

were not willing!" I suspect that it is not just Jewish people who have a hard time recognizing the good things that prophets speak to us about our inconsistencies in practice. It seems more a human condition.

Humor seeks to amend more than demean.

*

You proved your mettle, you proved your manhood, by the way you could wield an argument, crack a witticism, punch a line.

—REBECCA GOLDSTEIN, *MAZEL*, 221

Being the Son of God might limit your ability to have alone time and not be noticed, even if you're in Tyre, Gentile territory. Jesus enters a non-disclosed house, wants no one, no way, to know that he is there—but going unnoticed was not to happen (Mark 7:24). Such are the burdens of notoriety—and divinity, I suspect.

An unnamed woman, known only by her race, "Syro-Phoenician," wants Jesus to cast out a demon that is afflicting her daughter.

She falls at Jesus' feet, usually a sign of respect, and later calls him "Lord" when she addresses him. Her stance is one of determination and respect.[14] Jesus, however, does not respond in kind. Rather, Jesus answers with a *mashal*, a parable of sorts, regarding dogs not having priority at the dinner table. Taken at face value, Jesus seems to be comparing her *little* daughter to *little* dogs.

Maybe we should give Jesus a bit of slack with his untoward answer. He has come here to "get away from it all," we would say. Jesus has been up to his ears busy. In the previous couple of chapters in Mark, Jesus healed the Gerasene demoniac, restored a girl to life, healed another woman, was rejected in his hometown, sent the disciples on a mission trip, learned the loss of the life of his forerunner (John the Baptist), fed five thousand people lunch, walked on a stormy sea, healed a throng of people in Gennesaret, and argued with scribes and Pharisees.

Arguing with the scribes and Pharisees is probably the straw that broke this camel's back. To mix images, Jesus is dog-tired by my reckoning.

---

14. Gundry, *Commentary on the New Testament*, 167.

Even given that possibility, Jesus is seen to be either racist or sexist in his reply to this woman who seeks only healing for her daughter. (To be fair to Jesus, I doubt he has gone through HR training at his workplace.)

Proverbs, parables, folk tales, poems are *tests* of sorts. They venture alternatives rather than preach or decree. I would suggest that Jesus is not being rude, racist, or sexist. Rather, Jesus is *testing* where this woman's request originates. The story of this woman follows from Jesus telling his disciples that it is the things that come *from the heart* that defile a person (Mark 7:23).

Marcus points out the "incongruity that Jesus couches his refusal to help a child in a parable about the necessity of attending to children."[15] The woman, perhaps, sees the incongruity and calls Jesus on this point in her own parable: "Lord, yes but don't even the dogs under the table eat of the *children's* scraps?" Marcus says, "the woman 'steals the scene,' [by] her retort to Jesus [as] a delightful mixture of respectful address ("Lord"), seeming acceptance of an inferior position ("dogs"), *and daring repartee*."[16]

Jesus responds to her observation, no longer in parables, but with gracious healing. Jesus also shows

Harold Fisch, in A Remembered Future, *reflects on "historical archetypes" and makes the point that, whereas much of Western Literature concerns itself with that of "quest," we also find "testing" as a theme, one that runs throughout Scripture. Fisch says that the biblical notion of time is preeminently eschatological, whereas "quest" tends to be cyclical in nature. In testing we are challenged, and a response is necessary. Quests are rooted in "nature" while "trials/tests" are rooted in the biblical notion of covenant. Fisch says, "The essence of covenant is dramatic, the memory of an encounter in which responsibilities are undertaken and promises exchanged by both parties" (Fisch,* Remembered Future, *11). R. W. L. Moberly makes a similar observation: "[Testing] is necessary for human beings to become truly themselves, and so is for human good; testing may be a searing and demanding process; testing is the action of God in human life" (Moberly,* Bible, *105).*

---

15. Marcus, *Mark 8–16*, 468.

16. Marcus, *Mark 8–16*, 469 (emphasis added).

his admiration of her by immediately commending her saying and telling her to depart, since the demon has come out of her daughter (Mark 7:29).

The story goes that W. C. Fields, the great comedy actor, and notorious drinker and womanizer, is found by a friend reading the Bible. The friend asks him what he is doing. Fields replies, "I'm looking for loopholes."

In Luke 18:1–8 we hear another amusing story of a character, a woman, widowed, who displays a similar chutzpah *as the Syro-Phoenician woman. This widow shows remarkable grit in the face of the callousness of a judge towards her plight. The judge, we're told, "neither feared God nor had respect for people" (Luke 18:2b). Rather than a helpless, hopeless victim that might easily be her role in that society, she "assumes unusual responsibility for her own well-being," and presents a "shocking initiative" in the face of this injustice.[17] We're told that this widow "bothers" the judge, but Green says that it is better rendered "badgered" since she doesn't just "wear him out" but actually uses terminology from the world of boxing (though she doesn't display any violence).[18] So much for machismo. Green concludes that we may "learn from her the import of engaging in the quest for justice—even when that quest requires that one act outside the script."[19] Justice in the Bible is never portrayed as a blindfolded woman holding scales; rather let justice "roll down like waters, and righteousness like an everflowing stream (Amos 5:24). Humor seeks to tutor, not preach or coddle.*

The people of God that Jesus has been dealing with the past several chapters in Mark are people who seem to be looking for loopholes: How can I fulfill the rules?

This woman, however, isn't looking for a loophole. She's looking for healing, for grace.

The only outsiders in God's kingdom are those who think they deserve to be insiders or those who seek loopholes. *Mazel* seldom alights on loophole seekers, at least not graciously.

The woman acknowledges that she is little more than a dog in some people's eyes. She makes no claim on God; expects no special status. She, the consummate outsider, shows Jesus that she knows how far-reaching God's love is for humankind, for the whole cosmos, of which she is among the least respected.

17. Green, *Luke*, 640.

18. Green, *Luke*, 641.

19. Green, *Luke*, 641.

The demons have no power in God's kingdom, and there are not just crumbs, but bread enough for all—and also wine (cf. John 2:10, "But you have kept the good wine until now"). Humor makes loopholes superflous and allows grace to abound.

Laughter on the Way to the Cross

> After Christians had meditated upon the Crucifixion, never again could laughter be thoughtlessly seen by them . . . as a sign of simple joy and buoyant happiness.
>
> —M. A. SCREECH, *LAUGHTER AT THE FOOT OF THE CROSS*, 17

The word "humor" is derived from the Latin humor, *meaning "fluid" or "moisture." The four "humors" was a theory developed in antiquity to explain how the body functions, especially with respect to health and sickness. These humors were associated with fluids that moved within our bodies, but also with the seasons and even with temperaments. For example, a "sanguine" person generally has a ruddy complexion and is optimistic. Laughter on the way to the cross is dark humor writ large. Indeed, most would be hard-pressed to call it "humor" at all, unless we know something of this classical sense of humor as a mood that comes from our bodily fluids. It would indeed be "ill-humor" then.*

I start this chapter with a personal note, both a confession and an apology. I have lived a rather charmed, somewhat sheltered life. I have experienced loss and disappointments, to be sure. I sometimes use the word "devastating" to describe some of my experiences, but I do so knowing that I weaken the word for those who have truly been razed by persons or events in this life.

Some of this hurt in our lives comes through a general brokenness that seems to be part of being born in this world "under the sun": "Moreover I saw under the sun that in the place of justice, wickedness was there, and in the place of righteousness, wickedness was there as well" (Eccl 3:16). This presence of wickedness in Scripture is not glossed over, nor does it preclude laughter. Occasionally a hard-won joy becomes possible in such situations. For those who have experienced extremes of loss and pain, where some line has been crossed and there seems no way back, I ask forgiveness if I move too quickly from the laughter of derision to joy in these next two chapters.

These seminal stories that I explore in no way deny or trivialize such destructive experiences. They are neither easy to read nor easy to accept. Without these stories, however, faith seems anemic or, worse, a "Disney-faith." The distance between tears and laughter is traversed by God bringing healing to the perniciousness of the affliction experienced in the midst of this life *under the sun*.

*

> The moment Ahab saw Elijah he said, "So it's you, old troublemaker!" "It's not I who has caused trouble in Israel," said Elijah, "but you and your government."
>
> —1 KINGS 17B–18A, *THE MESSAGE*

He was a "troubler" to be sure, not the first to be so called, but certainly among the more notorious. Assuredly someone amongst them could quote—from memory, no doubt—a proverb or two in the event they needed a theological justification for what they were doing: "He that troubleth his own house shall inherit the wind . . ." (Prov 11:29a, KJV).

This proverb may apply to any number of characters in Scripture. My personal favorite is the prophet Micah. Micah chastises the prophets who chastise him (Mic 2:6–11). Elijah is another prime suspect for the title; Elijah's mocking of Baal gets him in hot water with Ahab and Jezebel (1 Kgs 18–19). Within the Wisdom tradition the "Preacher" unsettles all our comfortable ways and truths: "All is *hevel* [vaporous, absurd]," he admonishes us (Eccl 1:2).

Perhaps Terry Lindvall is correct when he says, "Laughter must purge before it can redeem."[1]

Disregard and disrespect towards those in leadership (kings, prophets) is obviously a dangerous endeavor. Those who walk the corridors of power generally try to rein in troublers with corrective measures: "A whip for the horse, a bridle for the donkey, and a rod for the back of fools" (Prov 26:3).

---

1. Lindvall, *God Mocks*, 5.

At the foot of the cross, there is only derision and brutality: "He trusts in God; let God deliver him now, if wants to" (Matt 27:43). As Screech says, "Even in translation the sneering laughter comes across like a slap on the face."[3] The prophet Isaiah said as much centuries before Jesus came on the scene: "I gave my back to those who struck me, and my cheeks to those who pulled out the beard; I did not hide my face from insult and spitting" (Isa 50:6).

Mocking laughter can be dangerous against God's prophets. When Elisha goes up to Bethel some boys from the local village come out to jeer the prophet. "Go away baldy," they yell at him. Elisha in turn curses them, and two she-bears come out of the woods and maul forty-two of the boys! This story has been troubling to both Jewish and Christian readers at least since Roman times (2 Kgs 2:23–25).[2]

*

In life as in death Jesus provoked the kind of laughter encapsulated in that verb *derideo*: he was scoffed at.

—M. A. SCREECH, *LAUGHTER AT THE FOOT OF THE CROSS*, 27

The four canonical Gospels present the trial and crucifixion of Jesus with their particular concerns and vocabulary. All four Gospels tell of Jesus being mocked, first by the Jewish authorities and then by the Roman authorities. The motivation for mocking Jesus differs among the various camps involved in the trial; the Jews are concerned with Jesus being a false *messiah* and a false *prophet* (Mark 14:61, 65), whereas the Romans think him a false *king* (Mark 15:2–3). Yet all four Gospels have a general agreement that Jesus was verbally and physically abused: accusations, mocking, ridiculing, spitting, and slapping were all employed by both the Jewish and Roman authorities.[4]

2. Fox, *Early Prophets*, 704.

3. Screech, *Laughter*, 17.

4. This mocking of Jesus by the Jewish and Roman authorities raises numerous exegetical and historical issues. I shall not attempt to sort through all these problems. Furthermore, I will focus the bulk of my comments on Mark. See Brown, *Death of the Messiah*, for a rather exhaustive examination of all four Gospels and the issues and options involved.

The satirical and ironical character of the acts have echoes elsewhere in Scripture. The slapping, spitting, and other forms of physical mistreatment are allusions to the prophecies of Isaiah regarding the "Suffering Servant" (in addition to Isa 50:6, see also Isa 53:7 and Ps 22). The Jewish and Roman authorities seem clueless as to these theological undertones of their acts, but the authors are keenly aware of it and expect attentive readers to notice them as well.

*

> For I hear many whispering: "Terror is all around! Denounce him! Let us denounce him!" All my close friends are watching for me to stumble.
>
> —JEREMIAH 20:10

After the Last Supper, while Jesus was praying in the garden of Gethsemane, a contingent arrives from "the chief priests, the scribes, and the elders" (Mark 14:43). Jesus is brought before Pilate and the Jewish authorities, the self-same authorities to whom Jesus came to proclaim the good news that God was once again at work in the lives of God's chosen people (Mark 1:1).

We are told upfront that the Jewish authorities were looking for testimony against Jesus, but they found none; we are also told that many gave false testimony and contradictory evidence against Jesus (Mark 14:55–56). The high priest asks Jesus about the various charges against him. Jesus, however, remains silent. Gundry notes that Jesus' double refusal to answer the questions ("but he kept silent, and he made no answer," Mark 14:61) emphasizes Jesus' refusal to admit guilt on these charges.[5]

When finally asked by the high priest if Jesus was the "Son of the Blessed One" (Mark 14:61), Jesus replies, "I am" and adds, "You will see the Son of Man seated at the right hand of the Power, and coming with the clouds of heaven" (cf. Ps 110:1 and Dan 7:13). Gundry observes that this addition indicates that Jesus will "not as now be subject to judgment by the Sanhedrin (Mark 14:62)."[6] While there is some ambiguity in Jesus' reply, these words leave little doubt of his guilt in the minds of his accusers.

5. Gundry, *Mark*, 885.

6. Gundry, *Mark*, 887.

At this statement the high priest makes a dramatic gesture, tearing his clothes and asking if they need any more evidence (Mark 14:61–64). Gundry makes the point that the "iterative" verbs ("were not finding" and "were testifying falsely") emphasize Jesus' innocence and the Sanhedrin's "failure to find true testimony."[7] Marcus observes, "The farcical logic of the Markan Sanhedrin trial, then, approaches that enunciated by the Red Queen, 'Sentence first—verdict afterwards.'"[8]

The scene before the Jewish authorities ends with, "Some began to spit on him, to blindfold him, and to strike him, saying to him, 'Prophesy!'" (Mark 14:65).

The verbal and physical abuse is troubling, but the most intriguing gesture may be "covering" Jesus' face and asking him to prophesy (Mark 14:65b). This action amounts to a variation on "blind man's bluff"—Can you guess who hit you? The assumption by the tormentors is that this should be a child's game for a true prophet. Brown argues that this game is a "burlesque" of Jesus' ability to prophesy.[9] Jesus had publicly said that he would destroy "this temple and raise it again in three days" (Mark 14:58). Brown comments, "Although [Jesus] can prophesy such marvelous things, has he the ability of prophesying demanded by a *child's game*?"[10]

If the authorities' threefold punishment of Jesus and the blindfold game were not enough, the scene ends with the guards taking Jesus and beating him as well (Mark 14:65b). All this indicates a *thoroughness* to the Jewish authorities' mockery and abuse.

---

7. Gundry, *Mark*, 884.

8. Marcus, *Mark 8–16*, 1017, citing Lewis Carroll, *Alice in Wonderland*, ch. 12.

9. Brown, *Death*, 575.

10. Brown, *Death*, 575 (emphasis added). In his analysis of this scene from all four Gospels, Brown freely uses the term "burlesque" and even "buffoonery" for the actions of both Jewish and Roman authorities. Brown closes his analysis by citing 1 Cor 1:23, "We preach Christ crucified, a stumbling block to the Jews [a 'false prophet'] and foolishness to the Greeks [a 'false king']."

Is there any time, night or day, that roosters do not crow?
—CICERO, QUOTED IN MARCUS, *MARK 8–16*, 1020

In Mark the scene shifts to the courtyard below where Peter is warming himself. A servant girl of the high priest says, "'You also were with Jesus, the man from Nazareth.' But he denied it, saying, 'I do not know or understand what you are talking about'" (Mark 14:66–68). Peter is confronted by another person, and again denies knowing Jesus. Mark tells us that Peter "began to curse, and he swore an oath, 'I do not know this man you are talking about.' At that moment the cock crowed for the second time. Then Peter remembered that Jesus had said to him, 'Before the cock crows twice, you will deny me three times.' And he broke down and wept" (Mark 14:71–72).

Marcus, citing Brown (*Death*), notes the scholarly investigation into the crowing of the cock that occurs when Peter outright denies Jesus a third time. Apparently the time of the crowing and even the presence of this animal in the courtyard of the high priest is in question. The cock crows because that was part of what Jesus said would happen, that Peter would deny Jesus three times before the cock crows twice (Mark 14:30). All that happens on this night is part of what needs to take place for the work of Christ to be complete. Marcus further observes that when the cock crowed this second time, Peter remembers Jesus' words about his denial: "All has been foreseen, even Peter's denial, but that faithless act is not the last word . . . the doors of repentance are always open."[11]

There is a stark contrast and sad irony that just when Jesus is confessing his messiahship, Peter refuses to confess that he is Jesus' disciple. Brown observes that this whole trial before the Jewish authorities "highlights finely and ironically the fulfillment of Jesus' prophecy" regarding his rejection.[12] Gundry says of Peter's denial, following as it does on the heels of this trial before the Jewish authorities, "Two down, one to go—Mark is counting" with respect to Jesus' prophecies of his betrayal and ultimate death.[13] Jesus is shown to be the true prophet that the Jewish authorities fear he might be.

11. Marcus, *Mark*, 1025.
12. Brown, *Death*, 887.
13. Gundry, *Mark*, 889.

Even though there is this smidgeon of hope in Mark's narrative about Jesus' arrest and trial (that Jesus had foretold all this that would happen before he would be vindicated), the picture is one where "the last remnant of Jesus' inner circle has now abandoned him and he has been condemned to death by the highest authority in Palestine."[14]

*

Funny is the opposite of not funny, and of nothing else.

—G. K. CHESTERTON, "ON MR. MCCABE
AND A DIVINE FRIVOLITY," 159

When morning breaks Jesus is "bound, led, and handed over" to Pilate by the Jewish leadership (Mark 15:1). Pilate queries Jesus about his charges, specifically, whether Jesus is "king of the Jews." Jesus answers, "You say so" (Mark 15:2). Pilate is *amazed* when Jesus offers no other response to the charge (Mark 15:5).

This awe that Pilate displays recalls Isa 53:7: "He was oppressed, and he was afflicted, yet he did not open his mouth; like a lamb that is led to the slaughter, and like a sheep that before its shearers is silent, so he did not open his mouth." Both the Jewish and Roman authorities have now pronounced Jesus' kingship in their inquiry, thus ironically confirming who this Jesus is. Marcus says, "It [Pilate's statement of Jesus' kingship] cheekily shifts the responsibility for a positive evaluation of Jesus' kingship onto Pilate."[15] Irony seems to reign, not the authorities.

The humiliation of Jesus continues as Pilate seeks to have Jesus released through a "loophole" that a prisoner could be released during festival time. Pilate asks the crowd if they want the "king of the Jews" to be released. They answer, "Crucify him!" When further queried, "What has he done?" they simply reply, "Crucify him!" Pilate, wanting to satisfy the crowd, has Jesus flogged and then hands Jesus over for crucifixion (Mark 15:1–15).

The disciples first, and now the crowds turn against Jesus. It seems safe to say that some in the crowd who were calling for Jesus' crucifixion were part of the crowd that, a week earlier, heralded Jesus with the acclamation, "Hosanna! Blessed is the one who comes in the name of the Lord! Blessed

14. Marcus, *Mark 8–16*, 1025.

15. Marcus, *Mark 8–16*, 1034.

is the coming kingdom of our ancestor David! Hosanna in the highest heaven!" (Mark 11:9–10).

As Marcus observes regarding the treatment before Pilate, "the bound and seemingly powerless Jesus is actually advancing toward holy-war victory."[16] However, there is still further mockery, scorn, and physical abuse before we see this castigation come to an end.

Jesus is turned over to his executioners, the Roman leaders and soldiers. Another triad introduces this phase of Jesus' mockery: Jesus is bound, led, and handed over (Mark 15:1). "Are you king of the Jews?" Pilate asks. Jesus replies, "*You* say so" (Mark 15:2).

This new trial is very similar to the trial by the Sanhedrin. Marcus notes that Jesus' words and action are not "calculated to induce sympathetic feelings," neither does Jesus employ "respectful rhetoric" such as "my lord."[17] Jesus is not helping his case here.

Yet, as Marcus further notes, Jesus replies "ironically in turn to Pilate's ironic question" to Jesus about his kingship, showing that Jesus seems "anything but powerless" in the face of the Roman authorities.[18] In the end, the inexorable cry for crucifixion is raised from the crowd and Jesus is led to the Roman soldiers who would carry out the execution.

✶

The merry world did on a day . . . / to meet together where I lay /and
all in sport to jeer at me.

—GEORGE HERBERT, "THE QUIP"

The Roman soldiers clothe Jesus in a purple cloak, a mocking sign of royalty, then carry this royal mocking further by crowning him with thorns and saluting him as "king of the Jews." They are not done yet. They further strike his head, spit, and kneel in "homage" before Jesus (Mark 15:16–20). All these actions "unwittingly" point to his identity as king.[19]

16. Marcus, *Mark*, 1035.

17. Marcus, *Mark*, 1034.

18. Marcus, *Mark*, 1033; irony subverting irony!

19. Marcus, *Mark*, 1046.

The next four verses are deftly narrated to mix verbal with "sartorial" mockery.[20] Gundry points out that the repeated hitting of his crown heaps insults on Jesus' thorny *crown*, the spitting heaps insults on his royal *robe*, and kneeling heaps insults on his *claim to kingship*.[21] All this is told in the "iterative perfect"—the action *unfurls* before us. Even *The Message* renders the soldiers' mockery with earthy language, "Bravo, King of the Jews!" and follows with "banging" his head "with a club," ending with the spitting and kneeling in mock worship (Mark 15:18–19).

Mark tells us that a "whole" cohort mocks and scourges Jesus (Mark 15:16). The numbers involved (from as little as eighty, perhaps, to eight hundred and more) stretch the imagination. Gundry remarks that attempts to limit or explain the numbers "may not hit on the historical truth; but they certainly miss Mark's point of emphasis."[22] Caricature is a tool for satire and irony. Mark is possibly satirizing the satiric acts of both the Jewish and Roman trials and actions by noting a *throng* of soldiers seems necessary in the event that this *solitary* person somehow outmaneuvers the Jewish and Roman leaders with their cohorts.

Gundry makes the point that this double mockery and denial of Jesus (by the Jewish leaders and the Romans) brings out the double fulfillment of Jesus' predictions regarding his own death: "By framing the challenge that Jesus prophesy, these two fulfillments *ironically* show him to be the prophet that the Sanhedrin think he is not."[23] Other ironies show themselves when the chief priests and scribes note that Jesus saved others but could not save himself (Mark 15:31) and when the brigands on the cross say is he not one of them—and therefore not a revolutionary king but another sort of king (Mark 15:32).[24]

The mockery has reached its climax with this scene. By including these little ironies, Mark (and the other evangelists) are dissemblers of sorts (*eiron* in Greek).

20. Gundry, *Mark*, 940.
21. Gundry, *Mark*, 940.
22. Gundry, *Mark*, 940.
23. Gundry, *Mark*, 888 (emphasis added).
24. Marcus, *Mark*, 1052.

Well, you know, darling ... there's such a thing as *mazel*.

—REBECCA GOLDSTEIN, *MAZEL*, 15

We've reached a climax of sorts in the previous comments; Jesus is sentenced to death on the cross. The mockery isn't quite over yet, however. There is a third mockery of Jesus as he hangs on the cross. It is not a person or a specific group that now mocks Jesus but a general disdain from various fronts: passersby deride Jesus by "shaking their heads" (citing Jesus' words that he would rebuild the temple in three days should it be destroyed), the chief priests and scribes continue to mock among themselves that he saved others but could not save himself, and even those crucified with him scorn Jesus (Mark 15:29–32). This third triad broadens the mockery from select authorities to include the *hoi polloi*, the general populace. Jesus' mockery is across the board.

Though these are triads, much as jokes are often shaped in *threes*, this triad does not have the shape of a joke. In a joke proper the third element acts or says something that undercuts the first elements. Here, rather, the final element in each triad and the final triad itself serve the same effect: this triad of triads confirms the *completeness* of the rejection and humiliation of Jesus. This is not a joke.

Mark 15 ends by noting that Jesus' time on the cross was rather short, that the death came quickly, that Jesus was properly buried in a new linen cloth, and that Jesus did not suffer the further indignity of hanging on the cross throughout the Sabbath (Mark 15:42–45).[25]

The rolling of the stone over the entrance of this tomb by Joseph of Arimathea prepares for the question of whether Jesus will have a proper burial after the Sabbath. The chapter ends by telling us that Mary Magdalene and Mary the mother of Jesus determine to ensure a proper burial for Jesus: "And Mary Magdalene and Mary the mother of Joses beheld where he was laid" (Mark 15:47).

This pause in the story is much like the story of Abraham and Isaac journeying up Mt. Moriah. Erich Auerbach describes that scene with these words: "The journey is like a silent progress through the indeterminate and the contingent, a holding of the breath, a process which has no present,

25. Gundry, *Mark*, 981.

which is inserted, like a blank duration between what has passed and what lies ahead, and which yet is measured: three days!"[26]

All this is stark, brutal abuse, neither trivialized nor glorified, but deftly narrated.

We are never prepared for "*mazel*-moments," but breath-holding times are opportunities for God to play with physics. *Mazel* is, after all, the "imp of metaphysics."

26. Auerbach, *Mimesis*, 10.

The Sowing of Tears

Where does their laughter come from? It comes from as deep a place
as tears come from, and in a way it comes from the same place. As
much as tears do, it comes out of the darkness of the world where
God is of all missing persons the most missed, except that it comes
not as an ally of darkness but as its adversary, not as a symptom of
darkness but as its antidote.

—FREDERICK BUECHNER, *TELLING THE TRUTH*, 55–56

In *Reversed Thunder*, Eugene Peterson writes what he calls a "pastoral
midrash" on the book of Revelation, the last book in Scripture. Peterson
sees the author as a visionary who tells us nothing we haven't already encountered in Scripture but tells us these truths in a way that we can see
them fresh.

The author in Rev 5 "weeps bitterly" because there is no one worthy
enough to open the scroll sealed with seven seals (Rev 5:1–4). However, the
lamb who was slaughtered is found worthy (Rev 5:9).

As the lamb opens each seal, various horses emerge: a red horse of
war, a black horse of famine, and a pale horse of sickness unto death (Rev
6:1–6). Peterson observes, "Nothing that we experience as evil is unnoticed
or unacknowledged. It is all out in the open."[1] It is the angels who must
stand ground against this evil (Rev 7:1).

Evil, Peterson says, is not explained and is not minimized; it is con-
tained, "bracketed between Christ and prayer."[2]

We see this pattern throughout Scripture in stories, prophetic words,
and psalms. We term the pattern in different ways: loss and restoration;
disaster and flourishing; death and resurrection.

1. Peterson, *Reversed Thunder*, 81.
2. Peterson, *Reversed Thunder*, 85.

The image of "exile and return" is a particularly concrete and powerful image of the cycle. The seminal story of the people of God in Egypt and the later exile and return from Babylon figure prominently in the stories, prophecies, and psalms of ancient Israel.

> Ps 137:1–3, *The Message*
>   Alongside Babylon's rivers
> we sat on the banks; we cried and cried,
> remembering the good old days in Zion.
>   Alongside the quaking aspens
> we stacked our unplayed harps;
>   That's where our captors demanded songs,
> sarcastic and mocking:
> "Sing us a happy Zion song!"

> Ps 126:1–3, *The Message*
>   It seemed like a dream, too good to be true,
> when GOD returned Zion's exiles.
>   We laughed, we sang,
> we couldn't believe our good fortune.
>   We were the talk of the nations—
> "GOD was wonderful to them!"
>   GOD *was* wonderful to us;
> we are one happy people.

Exile and return. God present in both.

Perhaps the most profound view of loss is found in Lamentations, which Ellen Davis calls "The Love Poetry of Disaster."[3] The book shows "the most prolonged, intense expression of grief and shock" in all of Scripture.[4] Lamentations is recited on "Tisha b'Av"[5] for those of the Jewish faith, and read during Holy Week for Christians. Davis says that in the "most extreme situations, the deepest act of sanity for a human

> *In the liturgical calendar Ps 126 occurs in both Lent and Advent. We always live between exile and return, tears and joy, the cross and resurrection (cf. van Harn and Strawn, Psalms, 327–29).*

---

3. Davis, *Opening*, 291.

4. Davis, *Opening*, 291.

5. "Ninth of Av" in the Jewish calendar (usually during July or August in the Gregorian calendar). This is a time of remembering the destruction of the temple in Jerusalem, a time of fasting and prayer.

being may be to mourn what God mourns. . . . Hearing Lamentations in liturgy may help us receive what spiritual writers of earlier centuries called the 'gift of tears.'"[6] Such cries from the depths open avenues for healing and restoration.

We see this pattern of loss and restoration in the parables of Jesus as well. The lost sheep, lost coin, lost son (Luke 15): all three parables end with joy as the sheep, coin, and son are found, come home, and are welcomed at the end (Luke 15:7,10, 32).

*

Scorn and derision never come in tears.

—WILLIAM SHAKESPEARE,
A MIDSUMMER NIGHT'S DREAM, 3.2.12

The mockery and crucifixion of Jesus is heinous. It is as if all the cruelty and savagery that ever was is concentrated in a single event; a rain forest in a single drop of water. Yet such dissoluteness gets played out over and over again, between countries, cities, villages, and even within households. Words like "abhorrent" and "iniquitous"—awful sounding words!—gloss over the reality of such evils.

We say, "I can't imagine . . ." but we do. We've heard stories, seen pictures; and too many have experienced it.

The scorn at the crucifixion seems fundamentally different from the scorn in Ps 2. The kings in Ps 2 seek to subjugate, whereas the leaders and soldiers in the Gospels seek to afflict and demean. There is no cleverness, no surprise in the actions of the perpetrators; their humor has no redemptive purpose; it is retributive only. They

> Should God have laughed from the heavens at those who mocked Jesus, as he did at those leaders in Psalm 2? Screech notes Erasmus who said there was no "toning down the Crowd's diasyrm [disparagement]." Erasmus goes on to say, "They called down destruction upon themselves and on their posterity. But Christ, more merciful towards them than they were to themselves, rejects no man from forgiveness provided that he repent. Many then in that crowd yelling, 'Take him! Crucify him!' later came to venerate the Cross of Christ."[7]

6. Davis, *Opening,* 297.

7. Screech, *Laughter,* 210.

are barbaric; *chasar-lev*, "empty hearted/headed." The kings in Ps 2 are immoral and the leaders and crowds in the Gospels are amoral. The difference is slight, I suspect, especially for those who have experienced such treatment. In either case it is a laughter devoid of joy.

The scorn at the cross allows neither blocking nor over-accepting; there is no jugglery, no circumvention. Jesus will over-accept, but only by going *through* the abuse; rather than a tit-for-tat, power versus power approach, Jesus "empties himself" of pretense to power as domination.[8]

Is the mockery and crucifixion of Jesus a "tragedy"? Tragedy, like comedy, cannot be reduced to something simple and knowable in the abstract. Rowan Williams notes that literary tragedy raises questions about "selfhood, intelligence . . . empathy . . . and hope" and how we confront issues of abiding importance, among other things.[9]

In telling—with such vivid detail!—the betrayal of Jesus, the Gospel writers do not gloss over the extent and breadth of human evil. Scripture doesn't minimize evil; it doesn't condone or rationalize it. It shows disgrace, agony, and death unflinchingly. Is it the lack of explanation that makes such things so . . . *loathsome*? Words pale; to put a name to it almost always moves the experience towards abstraction, the abyss of lived experience. Explanation seldom suffices.

> "The irreducible paradox is that in speaking of the worst that can be imagined or experienced, we discover our capacity to 'think' it—not to rationalize or minimize it, but to allow it to pose the question to us: what endures of our humanity?"
> —Williams, *Tragic*, 144

---

8. "On the cross Christ's body becomes the site where Rome's pretensions to dominion are overwhelmed by the power of God, a power revealed in weakness" (Fowl, *Philippians*, 99).

9. Williams, *Tragic*, 138.

Lord, who createdst man in wealth and store,
Though foolishly he lost the same,
Decaying more and more,
Till he became
Most poore:
With thee
O let me rise
As larks, harmoniously,
And sing this day thy victories:
Then shall the fall further the flight in me.

—George Herbert (d. 1633), "Easter Wings,"

The three women come to the tomb early, as the sun rises (Mark 16:2). This detail, as Marcus observes, reverses the darkness that comes over the earth at noon as Jesus hangs on the cross.[10] Marcus says, "In the Markan context, the ascent of the sun at Jesus' resurrection reverses the darkness of his crucifixion."[11] Once again, as Mark tells us this story, the women "are coming," so that we see the events unfolding before us, much as Mark did in telling the crucifixion of Jesus.

As the women approach the tomb, an obvious and enticing question emerges, "Who will roll the stone away?" Marcus notes that the verb "roll away" in the Septuagint occurs three times in Gen 29:3–10 where a small group "laments its ability to move [a stone], and the stone is shifted by divine intervention."[12] As the three women draw near to the tomb, they "are looking up," seeing "that the stone

The shape of "Easter Wings" is not mere decoration or cleverness. Herbert was both priest and poet; his poetry displays his gifts as priest, theologian, and as a creative poet whose use of words and images serves him to explore his faith. Here Herbert shapes his poem in the form of wings—larks' wings? The poem, in both words and shape, presents us with the paradox of Jesus' death and resurrection: sin led Jesus to become "most poore" but resurrection gives "flight" to us. This is the pattern of exile and return, of joy.

10. Marcus, *Mark 8–16*, 1083.

11. Marcus, *Mark 8–16*, 1083.

12. Marcus, *Mark 8–16*, 1080.

is rolled away." Mark also stresses the size of the stone; it is "very large" (Mark 16:4), further emphasizing the mysterious nature of the stone being rolled. Who, indeed, could have done this?[13] As readers we are drawn into this mystery and must wonder alongside the women.

This puzzlement leads us to experience the women's other emotions as the scene unfolds. There is a notable threefold progression of Mark's description of their responses. First the women are "alarmed" (v. 6). Then when the young man tells them to "go" (v. 7), they don't simply "go," they "went out quickly" and "fled" in "terror and amazement," underscoring their fear (Mark 16:8).

"Fear" is a typical response to theophanies and angelophanies in Scripture.[14] Furthermore, fear often expresses "wonderment," not lack of faith.[15] Much as we shared in the sorrow of the cross, we are to share this experience of *surprise* in what is happening in the resurrection.[16] Dead bodies don't get up and go.[17]

There is a breathlessness in this crowning *mazel*-moment.

*

But of this you can be sure. Whenever you find tears in your eyes,
especially unexpected tears, it is well to pay the closest attention.
. . . More often than not God is speaking to you through them of the
mystery of where you have come from and is summoning you to where
. . . you should go next.

—FREDERICK BUECHNER, *WHISTLING IN THE DARK*, 117

13. Gundry, *Mark*, 990.

14. Marcus, *Mark 8–16*, 1081. Recall when the angels tell Abraham and Sarah that Sarah will conceive and have a child in the spring, she also responds in fear when they address her as to why she laughed (Gen 18:15).

15. Gundry, *Mark*, 1015.

16. A good storyteller (especially, perhaps, in an oral culture) could heighten the effect of these words and actions through pacing, intonation, and so forth, much as Mark does through his storytelling skills.

17. Zombies, of course, are the exception. Lest you think the Bible makes no reference to zombies, consider: "And this shall be the plague with which the Lord will strike all the peoples that wage war against Jerusalem: *their flesh will rot while they are still standing on their feet, their eyes will rot in their sockets, and their tongues will rot in their mouths*" (Zech 14:12, ESV).

Whedbee talks of comedy having a "U-shaped plot."[18] The action un-folds with a downward movement, such as danger, affliction, etc., and then takes an unexpected turn upwards with some favorable outcome. A smile turns up, not down.

There is an obvious truth to Whedbee's observation. However, what is happening with the crucifixion and resurrection is only superficially the same as what happens with comedy. Yes, there is a "happy ending" as with all comedy. However, in these texts and actions, it's not simply a "smile" ending but a "joy" ending. What is razed is now raised. The ultimate incon-gruity after the cross is resurrection, a good experience, but not necessarily a comfortable one.[19]

Resurrection is the wresting back of life *through* death, not *in place of* death. The return to the promised land is *from* exile.

The cross and resurrection are not acts that cancel each other out, or mere symbols, but material acts by God that go beyond simply rebuild-ing what was decimated or finding what was lost. It is a *new* thing, a *new* temple, a *new* creation; it is a lost sheep carried back on the shoulders of the shepherd (Luke 15:1–7). This is a surprise beyond expectation and even imagination. It is a palpable act that personifies joy, a jubilance embodied by the work of God in the cosmos and in our lives. The cross is sacramental because what is endured becomes an occasion for grace. It is humor not merely as U-shaped plot, but humor as sacramental act.[20]

J. R. R. Tolkien in a letter to his son Christopher relates an experi-ence Tolkien had at a church service when the *Quarant'Ore*[21] was being observed. Tolkien speaks of "light" he observed suspended in a small mote; it was not a "thing" interposed between God and the creature, but "God's very attention itself, personalized." He goes on to say that it was not "recap-turable in clumsy language" and neither was the "great sense of joy" that accompanied the experience.[22]

---

18. Whedbee, *Comic Vision*, 7.

19. This observation seems also true with the combination of Pss 137 and 126, as also with certain parables of Jesus (e.g., Matt 13:31–33, 44–46).

20. See, e.g., Tomko, "Good Laugh," 312–31; Ballinger, *Poem as Sacrament*, 221–32.

21. A service where the Blessed Sacrament is on display for forty hours, honoring the time Jesus spent in the tomb from Good Friday until Easter Sunday. The service is held especially at the *Triduum* (the three days from Maundy Thursday through Good Friday and Holy Saturday). It can also be held at other feast times.

22. Tolkien, *Letters*, letter 89.

From this experience and a related story about a little boy who had a miraculous healing, Tolkien speaks of these "intrusions . . . into real or ordinary life, but they do intrude into real life, and so need ordinary meals and other results."[23] Tolkien goes onto to say that this story (of the boy) "with its apparent sad ending and then its sudden unhoped-for happy ending" deeply moved him. He connects these experiences with what he had been saying about fairy stories, for which he coined a term, "eucatastrophe": "the sudden happy turn in a story which pierces you with a joy that brings tears."[24]

For Tolkien the resurrection is the greatest eucatastrophe possible in the greatest fairy story—and produces the essential emotion: "Christian joy which produces tears because it is qualitatively so like sorrow, because it comes from those places where Joy and Sorrow are at one, reconciled, as selfishness and altruism are lost in Love."[25]

These experiences are emblematic, they speak to something deep within us and have the power to reconstruct how we think and live in the world. They are *sacramental*, they raise words and events beyond mere symbolism. Helena Tomko also speaks of the humor in Evelyn Waugh's novel *Helena* as not just sign or symbol, but as the material fact that undergirds what faith has taught her: "hers is a humor that does not mock or correct but instead seeks to heal and love."[26]

*

The world is charged with the grandeur of God.

—GERARD MANLEY HOPKINS, "GOD'S GRANDEUR" (POETRY-FOUNDATION.ORG/POEMS/44395/GODS/GRANDEUR)

Hopkins says that the world is "charged with the grandeur of God" only because he knows that in this world under the sun,

23. Tolkien, *Letters*, letter 100.
24. Tolkien, *Letters*, letter 100.
25. Tolkien, *Letters*, letter 100.
26. Tomko, "Good Laugh," 327.

Generations have trod, have trod, have trod;
And all is seared with trade; bleared, smeared with toil;
And wears man's smudge and shares man's smell: the soil
Is bare now, nor can foot feel, being shod.

Hopkins can hold these truths together because he knows that the mocking and cruelty Jesus endures becomes an occasion for grace, for laughter. It is not simply the laughter that a child has playing peek-a-boo, though that may be part of it, something we don't lose completely along the way. Rather it is the laughter that comes in *mazel*-moments where

There lives the dearest freshness deep down things;
And though the last lights off the black West went
Oh, morning, at the brown brink eastward, springs—
Because the Holy Ghost over the bent
World broods with warm breast and with ah! bright wings.

It is the laughter that follows our return from the far country, that finds the sheep that got lost and that blasted little coin dropped but now seen in a corner. It is exile and *return*.

Ellen Davis says that the psalms have the "particular genius of . . . instruct[ing] our feelings without negating them."[27] The pattern of exile and return plays out often within a particular psalm but most assuredly between one psalm and another. Having felt the force of Ps 137, we can feel the joy of Ps 126 perhaps with a deeper conviction. Parables also have this "particular genius." Missing the opportunity for such laughter in Scripture is truly lamentable. When we read Scripture with "but our foreheads,"[28] we limit occasions for the surprise of grace.

The psalms and parables don't preach at us so much as invite us into the story set before us; in doing so the stories instruct our

> "Sometimes the star is still. Sometimes she dances. She is Mary's star. Within that little pool of Wear she winks at me. I wink at her. The secret that we share I cannot tell in full. But this much I will tell. What's lost is nothing to what's found, and all the death there ever was, set next to life, would scarcely fill a cup." —Buechner, Godric, 96

---

27. Davis, *Wondrous Depth*, 21.

28. This image comes from *Evenor*, a book of stories by George MacDonald (nineteenth-century Scottish author and minister). I explore this in an essay, "The Ways We Read." *Radix* 36:4 (2012) 4–9.

experiences and move our hearts. Both psalms and parables are first stories, then theology.

If exile is all there is, who gives a fig for a penny, or for a sheep out in some ravine, or for a self-centered son who leaves home? Apparently God does because God is not content with exile. Exile is not where God desires us to dwell.

Rather, Ps 126 ends with a single term, *joy*: "Those who go out weeping . . . shall come home with shouts of joy" (Ps 126:6). And we "celebrate and *rejoice* because this brother of yours was dead and has come to life; he was lost and has been found" (Luke 15:24).

Joy is preeminently a sacramental term, a palpable term. Sacraments make present God with us ("Immanuel"). Hans Boersma entreats us to consider the entire cosmos as sacrament, "a material gift from God in and through which we enter into the joy of his heavenly presence."[29] The laughter of tears leads us there.

*

> You are newcomers here, and, as I guess,"
> said she, "my smiling in this spot elect
> to be the cradle of the human race
> May make you wonder, and perchance suspect;
> But the psalm *Delectasti* [Ps 92] gives you light
> to illumine your clouded intellect.
>
> —DANTE, *PURGATORY*, CANTO 38[30]

Jesus' trial, death, and resurrection make the move from brutality to rejoicing. This pattern is not what is "new" about the New Testament. It is the pattern of loss and restoration that runs throughout the story of God with God's creation. Exile and return, crucifixion and resurrection are graphic about the pain and despair and exuberant about the return and the joy. These experiences don't explain the stories but show the depths of God's pathos and healing.

29. Boersma, *Participation*, 9.

30. Sayers, *Purgatory*, 295, comments that now that Dante and his companions have heard these words from the Lady, "they will know better than to suppose that smiles and cheerful behavior are inappropriate in holy places."

The Christian Scriptures end with a vision of a "new heaven and a new earth" (Rev 21). A new Jerusalem comes down from heaven, and a "loud voice" from the throne says,

> See, the home of God is among mortals.
> He will dwell with them;
> they will be his peoples,
> and God himself will be with them;
> he will wipe every tear from their eyes.
> Death will be no more;
> mourning and crying and pain will be no more,
> for the first things have passed away. (Rev 21:3–4)

This promise and movement is familiar language to those who have followed the story from the beginning. The end is much the same as how it started. Ellen Davis marks a difference between the biblical account of creation and that of her neighbors. In the Babylonian account of creation, when the gods realized that maintaining the temple was a lot of work, they created humanity to do the "menial work of the cosmos."[31] In contrast, in the biblical account of creation, God is more "like a parent who delights in a child, God chooses our company for *no good reason at all*."[32]

Later, God chooses to dwell among his people in the wilderness (Exod 25:8). Davis draws a connection between Israel's time of slavery in Egypt and the construction of the tabernacle. The stories are of similar length and contrast two kinds of work. Pharaoh's work is slave work; tabernacle work is "godly and humane and thus fully consonant with God's creational and covenantal intentions."[33] The construction of the tabernacle is "healing work"; it is "Sabbath-oriented. . . . It proceeds from a disposition of the heart and the work of the hands."[34] Indeed, Moses even has to tell them to cease from work since there is more than enough (Exod 36:5–6). Davis makes this observation: "Just as with manna, there is such a thing as enough."[35]

31. Davis, *Wondrous Depth*, 59.
32. Davis, *Wondrous Depth*, 13 (emphasis added).
33. Davis, *Wondrous Depth*, 59.
34. Davis, *Wondrous Depth*, 61.
35. Davis, *Wondrous Depth*, 61.

This pattern of exile and return is prominent in the prophets of Israel also. The prophet Hosea uses particularly passionate language, for both the "exile"—their going away from God—and for "return"—when God draws them back.

Peter and The Great Escape:
Berger says, "For it is not so much that one should believe because something is absurd, but rather that one should be led toward faith by the perception of absurdity" (Berger, Redeeming Laughter, 183).

It's an unbelievable story. Even he didn't believe it. He was sleeping, "double-chained and sandwiched between two soldiers."[36] Someone (an angel, we're told) smote him on his side to wake up. He wraps himself in his cloak and follows his liberator. He passes a couple of guards and exits through the gate, which opens "of its own accord" (Acts 12:10).[37] Once outside the gate, the angel departs immediately; its job is done (Acts 12:10).

Now that Peter was free, he goes to Mary's house (the mother of John Mark). Many of his friends were gathered there, praying for him. Rhoda goes to answer the door and upon hearing his voice beats-feet back to the group to tell them that Peter was there—at the door!! None of them believe her, of course, any more than Peter had believed that he was participating in a prison-break.

"All this time poor Peter was standing out in the street, knocking away" (Acts 12:16, The Message).

There was, as you might expect, much clamor over all that was happening right in front of them. Easy to deny—unless you were there!

"Everyone laughs in the future tense, for laughter reverberates with hope: It announces that the world is all right after all, and that it will continue, in its wobbly, quirky, unpredictable way." —Sanders, Sudden Glory, 32

Fisch, commenting on the passion God has for his people, says of this pattern in Hosea, "It is the poetry of love and estrangement, but neither can be entertained without the other. That is the special agony of Hosea. An angry God . . . is nevertheless haunted by his own unsubjugated affections."[38]

---

36. Gundry, Commentary on the New Testament, 511.

37. Gundry notes that the word used in this passage comes down into English as "automatically" (Gundry, Commentary on the New Testament, 511).

38. Fisch, Poetry, 140.

He follows this with, "[By the end of the book] the love of God has marvelously found its voice . . . flooding it with tears, with dew and rain."[39]

Hosea expresses with a deep pathos

> I will heal their disloyalty;
> I will love them freely,
> for my anger has turned from them.
> I will be like the dew to Israel;
> he shall blossom like the lily,
> he shall strike root like the forests of Lebanon.
> His shoots shall spread out;
> his beauty shall be like the olive tree,
> and his fragrance like that of Lebanon.
> They shall again live beneath my shadow,
> they shall flourish as a garden;
> they shall blossom like the vine,
> their fragrance shall be like the wine of Lebanon. (Hos 14:4–7)

Ellen Davis observes, "The prophetic trajectory in the Bible tends towards hope, the kind of difficult yet realistic hope that is born of a full reckoning with the dimensions of infidelity and disaster."[40]

The story of creation ends with blessing (Gen 1:28). The story of the construction of the tabernacle ends with blessing: "When Moses saw that they had done all the work just as the Lord had commanded, he blessed them" (Exod 39:43). The promises of return from exile culminate with blessings (Jer 31:23; Isa 65:23). The Christian Scriptures similarly end with a blessing: "The grace of the Lord Jesus be with all the saints. Amen" (Rev 22:21).

So it is *for no good reason at all* we laugh with joy for this gift of life bestowed on us from a God who spoke the cosmos into being, the *Torah* on Mt. Sinai, the Beatitudes on the Mount, and cautioned us time and again, "Do not fear, for I am with you, do not be afraid, for I am your God" (Isa 41:10).

---

39. Fisch, *Poetry*, 156.
40. Davis, *Prophecy*, 156.

The Lord's Emojis
(Vignette)

The idea of sacrament—an outward sign elevated into
something else, *the ordinary made into occasions of grace*—is
essential. It becomes a way of thinking about the world, rather
than just the way a religion is run.

—ALICE MCDERMOTT, "INTERVIEW," *IMAGE* 52

Priests have sacerdotal functions in the life of the people of God. They
are to issue God's *benefaction*, the blessings of the Lord, to the people:

> The Lord spoke to Moses, saying: Speak to Aaron and his sons,
> saying, Thus you shall bless the Israelites: You shall say to them,
> "The Lord bless you and keep you; the Lord make his face to shine
> upon you, and be gracious to you; the Lord lift up his countenance
> upon you, and give you peace." So they shall put my name on the
> Israelites, and I will bless them. (Num 6:22–27)[1]

This is a remarkable statement of Divine well-being towards the people. It expresses six core actions by God alone on behalf of the people: "The
Lord . . . bless *and* keep, shine *and* be gracious, lift up his countenance *and*
give peace."

As one would expect, this blessing shows up elsewhere in Scripture.
These words are as recognizable to the people of God as an emoji is to users
of social media today. For example, Ps 4 is a plea for God to intervene in a
time of distress. Peppered throughout the psalm are pieces and allusions to
the priestly blessing:

---

1. The following reflection was prompted by an article by Michael Fishbane, "Form
and Formulation of the Priestly Blessing."

Be gracious to me, and hear my prayer (v. 1)
. . . Let the light of your face shine on us, O Lord (v. 6)
. . . I will both lie down and sleep in peace. (v. 8)

Fishbane says that this psalm serves as a "theological matrix and as its ideational touchstone"[2] for the priestly blessing. The people of God expected the Lord to be a source of safety and blessing to them.

The priestly blessing is rich and powerful. It has a stair-step form, the first line being the shortest, the second a bit longer, and the final line longest of all. The words can also be read in different ways. The blessing has three distinct breaks in the lines, each with two "action" words. Are there six separate actions? That is, the "and" could mean "this *and* that." It could, however, also mean "this *is* that": the Lord's blessing *keeps* us, the shining *is* grace, countenance *results* in peace. This second option views the blessing as three blessings, not six. These are fun questions to ponder; either way, the blessing stands as the primary promise of God to the people.

The blessing ends with a clear comment that, though the priests articulate the blessing, they are not the source of the blessing. It is the Lord who blesses the people.[3]

★

If humour tells you something about who you are, then it might be a reminder that you are perhaps not the person you would like to be.

—SIMON CRITCHLEY, *ON HUMOUR*, 75

Alongside the blessing, of course, were certain expectations of the people. If they were to be God's people, they were expected to act like it! After delivering the people from slavery in Egypt, God says these words to Moses to convey to the people: "You have seen what I did to the Egyptians, and how I bore you on eagles' wings and brought you to myself. Now therefore, if you obey my voice and keep my covenant, you shall be my treasured possession out of all the peoples. Indeed, the whole earth is mine, but you shall be for me a priestly kingdom and a holy nation" (Exod 19:4–6).

2. Fishbane, "Priestly Blessing," 116.
3. Fishbane, "Priestly Blessing," 115–21.

As could be predicted, the people had a few lapses in these behavioral expectations. The prophet Malachi delivers a rather harsh critique of the priestly behavior in the post-exilic period. After many years of lapses, he inverts the blessing, especially for those of us who are "professionally religious." Fishbane calls it an "exegetical transformation" of the blessing; the prophet "with great ironic force" negates the blessings.[4] The priests have "despised" the name of the Lord (Mal 1:6) and otherwise besmirched the benefits of the blessing by their words and actions. Fishbane says, that the sacerdotal language is "systematically inverted and desecrated" through a series of puns that exposes the "liturgical mockery" of the priestly actions in Malachi's day. The actions of the people result in an "anti-blessing."[5]

> A son honors his father. . . . If then I am a father, where is the honor due me? . . . O priests, who despise my name. You say, "How have we despised your name?" By offering polluted food on my altar. And you say, "How have we polluted it?" By thinking that the Lord's table may be despised. . . . Try presenting that to your governor; will he be pleased with you or show you favor? . . . The fault is yours. . . . Oh, that someone among you would shut the temple doors, so that you would not kindle fire on my altar in vain! I have no pleasure in you . . . and I will not accept an offering from your hands. . . . "What a weariness this is," you say, and you sniff at me . . . You bring what has been taken by violence or is lame or sick, and this you bring as your offering! Shall I accept that from your hand? says the Lord. (excerpts from Mal 1:6–13)

The prophet does not mince words here—but he does "play" with them in his diatribe against the priests. The priests were to beseech the Lord (Mal 1:9) but in fact this action is countered when they *besmirch* the Lord's name by their actions (Mal 1:12).[6] The priestly language is "desacralized and their actions are cursed" and those whose job it was to bear the priestly blessing "could not have missed the exegetical irony and sarcastic nuance of the prophet's speech."[7]

Those of us who are professionally religious do not get a free pass on the things pertaining to God. Indeed, we are often the source of much vexation for the Lord.

4. Fishbane, "Priestly Blessing," 118.

5. Fishbane, "Priestly Blessing," 119.

6. The Hebrew words sound alike in Hebrew; Malachi is making a pun with these words, "You should be doing 'x' but you're really doing 'z.'"

7. Fishbane, "Priestly Blessing," 119.

You might think that if they [the priests] desired to bless Israel
they would be blessed and that if they did not, they would not be
blessed? The Torah states, "And I will bless them." Willy-nilly "I will
bless them" from heaven.

—SIFRI ZOTA, QUOTED IN LEIBOWITZ,
STUDIES IN BAMIDBAR, 62

Patrick Miller quotes Bonhoeffer as saying, "I should like to speak
of God, not on the borders of life, but at its center, not in weakness but
in strength, not therefore in man's suffering and death, but in his life and
prosperity."[8]

This sentiment of Bonhoeffer resonates with me. However, God's sig-
nature blessing over the people of God comes not after they have entered
the promised land and after they built the temple, but comes rather in the
desert, in the midst of the "deterioration" of the generation that God had
delivered from Egypt. As Ellen Davis notes, Leviticus and the Pauline cor-
pus are the "richest sources of insight into the phenomenon of the religious
failure of a whole people."[9]

Furthermore, the most concrete sign of God's favor comes through a
pagan prophet, not Moses, Aaron, or Miriam. That story is told in Numbers
22–24.

King Balak of Moab seeks the assistance of Balaam, prophet *extrao-
dinaire*, to curse the "horde" of Israelites passing through Moab on their
way to the promised land. Balaam says that he can only do what God tells
him, but he is willing to inquire of God (Num 22:8). God tells Balaam not
to curse the Israelites for "they are blessed" (Num 22:12). Balak comes back
with more incentives and Balaam goes to inquire once more, duly noting
again that he can only do what the Lord tells him. This time the Lord allows
him to go, but Balaam is also told to do only what the Lord tells him (Num
22:20).

Balaam sets out "early in the morning" (Num 22:21); God immediately gets mad at him (Num 22:22). On the surface this seems a bit capricious on God's part since God has just given Balaam permission to go.

8. Miller, "Blessing," 251.

9. Davis, *Opening*, 83.

The phrase "early in the morning" might be the key. This same phrase is used of Abraham when he and Isaac go up the mountain to sacrifice Isaac (Gen 22:3). Both stories share the theme of "testing." Is Balaam being tested much as Abraham was being tested in Gen 22? Will Balaam, this famous pagan prophetic, truly do *only* what God tells him? Getting up "early in the morning" suggests intention.

Balaam learns his lesson the way most of us do, the hard way. When the beast of burden *sees* the angel standing before them, the donkey stops. Balaam, rightly according to Prov 26:3, strikes the donkey: "A whip for the horse, a bridle for the donkey, and a rod for the back of fools." The donkey gives the famous prophet a "what for" at the end of the scene: "'Am I not your donkey, which you have ridden all your life to this day? Have I been in the habit of treating you this way?' And [Balaam] said, 'No'" (Num 22:30).

This parable of Balaam and "Jenny"[10] is an inversion of our normal expectations. In this parable, the donkey—seeing the danger ahead that the prophet Balaam doesn't see—is the faithful servant. Balaam the prophet, on the other hand, doesn't see the angel in the road. Balaam corresponds more to how the people of God are often portrayed in the biblical stories, just as likely to be unseeing and of questionable faithfulness.

"Balaam's obedience as a prophet is being tested, and the appropriate response is to laugh at the unseeing prophet."[11] An observant reader may well ask, "Who am I?" in this story.

Balaam learns his lesson the hard way, but he does learn it. Though Balak continues to entice him to do otherwise (Num 23–24), the prophet goes on the bless the people of God:

> [H]ow fair are your tents, O Jacob,
> your encampments, O Israel!
> Like palm groves that stretch far away,
> like gardens beside a river,
> like aloes that the Lord has planted,
> like cedar trees beside the waters.
> Water shall flow from his buckets,
> and his seed shall have abundant water. (Num 24:5–7)

Davis says, "Divine faithfulness ultimately trumps human ingratitude, doubt, and human presumption, the forms of faithlessness set forth in

10. "Jenny" is another term used for a donkey.

11. See Petrotta, "Balaam," 295.

the narratives of Numbers."[12] In *Godric*, Buechner's novel about a twelfth-century British saint, the character Godric says, as he reflects upon his life, "When I deserved it least, God gave me most."[13]

Total surprise and undeserving favor are the willy-nilliness of God's blessings. It is an "embodied and enacted spirituality."[14] Thank God—and smile, ear to ear.

---

12. Davis, *Opening*, 93.

13. Buechner, *Godric*, 144.

14. Davis, *Opening*, 63.

Reinhold Niebuhr on Humor and Faith
(Vignette)

I'm not afraid of death, I just don't want to be there
when it happens.

—WOODY ALLEN

Niebuhr says that there is "no laughter in the holy of holies," though it does have the capacity to "stand outside of life."[1] Rather, laughter is a prelude to faith and the beginning of prayer also.

Laughter, he goes on to say, can't deal with the fundamental incongruities of life where humanity's position is "so great yet so small, so significant and yet so insignificant."[2] He says, "The contradiction between judgement and mercy cannot be resolved by humour but only by vicarious pain."[3] He concedes that there is an "echo of the sense of humour" in the recognition that mercy and justice can be reconciled, but humor cannot supply that reconciliation.[4]

Finally, he also recognizes that philosophy likewise cannot bridge that chasm.[5]

Niebuhr's points are well-taken. I'm also not sure that humor ever seeks to rise to that level of force. Niebuhr recognizes that truth, I think,

---

1. Niebuhr, "Faith," 49.
2. Niebuhr, "Faith," 50.
3. Niebuhr, "Faith," 52.
4. Niebuhr, "Faith," 54.
5. Niebuhr, "Faith," 56.

when he says that humor is more profound than philosophy since humor recognizes the incongruities without devouring them into something else.[6]

What humor may do—and often does quite well—is to devour our "isms," all those things we cling to for support or as avoidance of the profound incongruities of life (whatever we call them). I think Niebuhr is correct about the fundamental incongruity knowing that justice and mercy must be reconciled, and for all our insignificance in this vast universe, there appears to be something profound about our ability to recognize that disparity.

Humor desacralizes our warm, yet truly false idols. Humor may not get us through that door of reconciliation, but it lets us see that there is a door and not a wall or, worse, a void.

6. Niebuhr says philosophy devours "incongruity into reason" ("Humor and Faith," 59–60).

The Sum of It All

I could tell you a great deal more concerning them all, but I have already told more than is *good for those who read but with their foreheads.*

—GEORGE MACDONALD, "THE WISE WOMAN," 115
(EMPHASIS ADDED)

Two things stand out to me as I look back over these reflections on humor in Scripture. The first is how we read; the second is the role that humor can play in a faith journey.

MacDonald's comment about forehead reading reminds me of what C. S. Lewis wrote in a little book, *An Experiment in Criticism.* Lewis offers this image: On the one hand, we can read in a leisurely fashion, like riding a bike on a country road. On the other hand, we can add a motor to our bike and see how fast we can get from one point to the next.

Lewis argues that books should be judged on the *readings they invite.*

Sarah making a quip about biology when God speaks theology is the classic stuff of humor where the characters crisscross in their views of what is or is not possible. When the Syro-Phoenician woman makes a riposte to Jesus' comment about dogs, I can't help but see Jesus smile.

A second thing that strikes me as I come to these final thoughts is the role humor can play in a faith. Kierkegaard famously says that humor is the last stage of existential awareness before faith. There is quite a bit to ponder in this assertion. We catch a glimpse of what he is thinking when Kierkegaard looks at the story of Abraham and Isaac in Gen 22 (the *Aqedah*, the "binding" of Isaac). Abraham is instructed by God to sacrifice his son, "thine only son Isaac, whom thou lovest" (Gen 22:2, KJV).

Abraham does not question God in this story, as he did before Isaac was born; neither does he try to bargain with God, as he did over Sodom and Gomorrah.[1] Rather, Abraham sets off "early in the morning" (Gen 22:3) to Mt. Moriah, an act that seems to disregard normal ethical behavior. Thus Abraham stands "in absolute relation to the absolute," Kierkegaard says.[2] Faith is the distance between staying at home and journeying to Moriah.

With humor we stand between the play of two worlds, one straightforward and one catawampus. We have to make some sense of it. These stories of humor have shown us that we can argue and even bargain with God. We can also laugh, either at God or with God. When we laugh, we see the world a bit differently, having traversed the gap between the initial proposal and the outcome where balance is restored.

> *"Funny," Nuala said without humor. "Well, it is kind of funny," Lucas said, "in a dreadful sort of way." "Funny," said Nuala, "unless it happens to you." Lucas raised his glass in salute. "Someday," he proclaimed, "Somewhere, somehow— everything will be funny for everyone."*
> *—Robert Stone, Damascus Gate, 243*

Humor is not faith, but it gives us practice in dealing with that space between the contradictions and irregularities of our lives, and the trust that "alle manner of thinge shalle be wel" (Julian of Norwich).

To read a scriptural story with an expectation that all will be well is a generous act to make towards a text and a prelude to faith, as Kierkegaard suggests.

*

After all these considerations of humor and how it plays out in concrete situations and texts, the last word on the subject will always be, "Well, I thought it was funny . . ."

I think that sums up what I've been saying about humor. There are strategies in humor, different functions of the trope, lots of ambiguity, and disagreements about what purpose humor may serve. In the end, though, there is one thing necessary: I thought it was funny. And if there be any grace, then the One who sits in the heavens laughs *with* us.

Amen.

---

1. The story is told in Gen 18:23–32. Abraham *negotiates* with God over the fate of the people of Sodom and Gomorrah.

2. Kierkegaard, *Fear and Trembling*, 122.

Select Bibliography

Adams, Douglas. *The Prostitute in the Family Tree*. Louisville: Westminster John Knox, 1997.

Addison, Joseph. *Essays in Criticism and Literary Theory 2*. Edited by John Loftis. Northbrook, IL: AHM, 1975.

Allen, Woody, dir. *Hannah and Her Sisters*. 1 hour 47 min. Orion Pictures, 1986.

———. *Sleeper*. 1 hour 29 min. United Artists, 1973.

———. *Stardust Memories*. 1 hour 29 min. United Artists, 1980.

Alter, Robert. *The World of the Biblical Narrative*. New York: HarperCollins, 1992.

Auerbach, Erich. *Mimesis: The Representation of Reality in Western Literature*. Princeton: Princeton University Press, 1953.

Ballinger, Philip A. *The Poem as Sacrament: The Theological Aesthetic of Gerard Manley Hopkins*. Louvain: Peeters, 2000.

Belloc, Hillaire. *The Path to Rome*. Long Prairie, MN: Neumann, 1983.

Benigni, Roberto, dir. *Life Is Beautiful*. 2 hours 2 min. Miramax, 1997.

Berger, Peter. "Christian Faith and the Social Comedy." In *Holy Laughter: Essays on Religion in the Comic Perspective*, edited by M. Conrad Hyers, 123–33. New York: Seabury, 1969.

———. *Redeeming Laughter*. Berlin: de Gruyter, 1997.

Berlin, Adele. *Esther*. The JPS Bible Commentary. Philadelphia: JPS, 2001.

Berlin, Adele, and Marc Zvi Brettler, eds. *The Jewish Study Bible: Jewish Publication Society Tanakh Translation*. New York: Oxford University Press, 1999.

Boersma, Hans. *Heavenly Participation: The Weaving of a Sacramental Tapestry*. Grand Rapids: Eerdmans, 2011.

Brown, Raymond E. *The Death of the Messiah: From Gethsemane to the Grave; A Commentary on the Passion Narratives in the Four Gospels*. Vol. 1. New Haven: Yale University Press, 1998.

Buckley, F. H. *The Morality of Laughter*. Ann Arbor: University of Michigan Press, 2003.

Buechner, Frederick. *Godric*. San Francisco: Harper & Row, 1980.

———. "Journey to Wholeness." *Theology Today* 49 (1993) 454–63.

———. *The Longing for Home*. San Francisco: HarperCollins, 1996.

———. *Telling the Truth: The Gospel as Tragedy, Comedy, and Fairy Tale*. San Francisco: Harper & Row, 1977.

———. *Whistling in the Dark: A Doubter's Dictionary*. San Francisco: HarperCollins, 1993.

———. *Wishful Thinking: A Seeker's ABC*. San Francisco: HarperCollins, 1993.

Calvin, John. *Commentaries on the First Book of Moses Called Genesis*. Grand Rapids: Baker, 1979.

Calvino, Italo. *Cosmicomics*. San Diego: Harvest, 1965.

Carroll, Lewis. *Alice in Wonderland and Through the Looking Glass*. Illustrated by John Tenniel. Illustrated Junior Library. New York: Grosset & Dunlap, 1984.

Carroll, R. P. "Is Humour Also Among the Prophets?" In *On Humour and the Comic in the Hebrew Bible*, edited by Yehuda Thomas Radday and Athalya Brenner, 169–90. Sheffield: Almond, 1990.

Chapman, Stephen B. *1 Samuel as Christian Scripture: A Theological Commentary*. Grand Rapids: Eerdmans, 2016.

Charry, Ellen T. *By the Renewing of Your Minds: The Pastoral Function of Christian Doctrine.*Oxford: Oxford University Press, 1997.

———. *God and the Art of Happiness*. Grand Rapids: Eerdmans, 2010.

———. "Lead Us into Joy." *The Anglican* (July 2002) 17–19.

Chesterton, G. K. *The Collected Works of G. K. Chesterton*. Edited by George J. Marlin et al. 35 vols. San Francisco: Ignatius, 1986.

———. "Heretics." In *The Collected Works of G. K. Chesterton*, edited by George J. Marlin et al., 1:157–66. San Francisco: Ignatius, 1986.

———. "On Mr. McCabe and a Divine Frivolity." In *The Collected Works of G. K. Chesterton*, edited by George J. Marlin et al., 1:157–66. San Francisco: Ignatius, 1986.

———. "On the Wit of Whistler." In *The Collected Works of G. K. Chesterton*, edited by George J. Marlin et al., 1:167–73. San Francisco: Ignatius, 1986.

Childs, Brevard S. *Isaiah: A Commentary*. Philadelphia: Westminster John Knox, 2000.

———. *Memory and Tradition in Israel*. London: SCM, 1962.

Cohen, Ted. "And What If They Don't Laugh?" In *The Anatomy of Humor*, edited by Toby Garfitt et al., 86–92. Studies in Comparative Literature 8. London: Legenda, 2005.

———. *Jokes: Philosophical Thoughts on Joking Matters*. Chicago: University of Chicago Press, 1999.

———. *Serious Larks: The Philosophy of Ted Cohen*. Chicago: University of Chicago Press, 2018.

Contino, Paul. "Interview with Alice McDermott." *Image* 52 (2007) 61–72.

Critchley, Simon. *On Humour*. London: Routledge, 2002.

Crystal, Billy, dir. *Mr. Saturday Night*. 1 hour 59 min. Columbia Pictures, 1992.

Davenport, Guy. *Every Force Evolves a Form*. Berkeley: North Point, 1987.

———. *The Hunter Gracchus and Other Papers on Literature and Art*. London: Routledge, 2002.

Davidson, Robert. *The Vitality of Worship: A Commentary on the Book of Psalms*. Grand Rapids: Eerdmans, 1998.

Davies, Robertson. *The Cunning Man*. New York: Viking, 1995.

Davis, Ellen. *Biblical Prophecy: Perspectives for Christian Theology, Discipleship, and Ministry*. Louisville: Westminster John Knox, 2014.

———. *Opening Israel's Scriptures*. Oxford: Oxford University Press, 2019.

———. *Proverbs, Ecclesiastes, and Song of Songs*. Louisville: Westminster John Knox, 2000.

———. *Scripture, Culture, and Agriculture: An Agrarian Reading of the Bible*. Cambridge: Cambridge University Press, 2008.

———. *Wondrous Depth: Preaching the Old Testament*. Louisville: Westminster John Knox, 2005.

Denny, David. *Man Overboard: A Tale of Divine Compassion.* Eugene, OR: Wipf & Stock, 2013.

Douglas, Mary. "The Social Control of Cognition: Some Factors in Joke Perception." *Man,* New Series 3 (1968) 361–76.

Eastwood, Clint, dir. *Heartbreak Ridge.* 2 hours 10 min. Warner Bros., 1986.

Elbogen, Ismar. *Jewish Liturgy: A Comprehensive History.* Translated by Raymond P. Scheindlin. Philadelphia: Jewish Publication Society, 1993.

Ellis, David. *Shakespeare's Practical Jokes: An Introduction to the Comic in His Work.* Lewisburg: Bucknell University Press, 2007.

Fisch, Harold. "The Hermeneutic Quest in *Robinson Crusoe.*" In *Midrash and Literature,* edited by Geoffrey H. Hartman and Sanford Burdick, 213–35. New Haven: Yale University Press, 1989.

———. *Poetry with a Purpose: Biblical Poetics and Interpretation.* Bloomington: Indiana University Press, 1990.

———. "Reading and Carnival: On the Semiotics of Purim." *Poetics Today* 15:1 (1994) 55–74.

———. *A Remembered Future: A Study in Literary Mythology.* Bloomington: Indiana University Press, 1984.

Fishbane, Michael. "Form and Formulation of the Priestly Blessing." *Journal of the American Oriental Society* 103:1 (1983) 115–21.

Fowl, Stephen. *Idolatry.* Waco: Baylor University Press, 2019.

———. *Philippians.* Grand Rapids: Eerdmans, 2005.

Fox, Everett. *The Early Prophets: Joshua, Judges, Saul and David.* Schocken Bible 2. New York: Schocken, 2014.

———. *The Five Books of Moses: Genesis, Exodus, Leviticus, Numbers, Deuteronomy.* Schocken Bible 1. New York: Schocken, 1995.

Fox, Michael V. *Proverbs 1–9.* Anchor Bible 18A. New Haven: Yale University Press, 2006.

———. *Proverbs 10–31.* Anchor Bible 18B. New Haven: Yale University Press, 2009.

Frankel, Ellen. *The Five Books of Miriam: A Woman's Commentary on the Torah.* San Francisco: HarperCollins, 1998.

Freeman, Tzvi. "What Is Chutzpah? And Is It Good or Bad?" https://www.chabad.org/library/article_cdo/aid/1586271/jewish/Chutzpah.htm.

Freud, Sigmund. *Jokes and Their Relation to the Unconscious.* Translated by James Strachey. New York: Norton, 1963.

Goldingay, John. *Psalms I: Psalms 1–41.* Grand Rapids: Baker, 2008.

Goldstein, Rebecca. *Mazel.* New York: Penguin, 1995.

Gordis, Robert. *Koheleth: The Man and His World.* 3rd ed. New York: Schocken, 1973.

Gouder, M. D. *Midrash and Lection in Matthew.* The Speaker's Lectures in Biblical Studies, 1969–71. London: SPCK, 1974.

Greenberg, Moshe. *Ezekiel 1–20.* Anchor Bible 22. Garden City, NY: Doubleday, 1983.

Gundry, Robert. *Commentary on the New Testament.* Peabody, MA: Hendrickson, 2010.

———. *Mark: A Commentary on His Apology for the Cross; Chapters 9–16.* Grand Rapids: Eerdmans, 2000.

———. *Matthew: A Commentary on His Literary and Theological Art.* Grand Rapids: Eerdmans, 1982.

Halpern, Baruch. "The Assassination of Eglon: The First Locked-Room Murder Mystery." *Bible Review* 4:6 (1988) 33–44.

Hampl, Patricia. "In the Belly of the Whale." In *Out of the Garden: Women Writers on the Bible*, edited by Christine Buchman and Celina Spiegel, 289–300. New York: Ballantine, 1994.

Handy, Lowell K. *Jonah's World: Social Science and the Reading of Prophetic Story*. BibleWorld. London: Equinox, 2007.

Hyers, M. Conrad. *Holy Laughter: Essays on Religion in the Comic Perspective*. New York: Seabury, 1969.

Jemelity, Thomas. *Satire and the Hebrew Prophets*. Literary Currents in Biblical Interpretation. Louisville: Westminster John Knox, 1992.

Jonsson, Jakob. *Humour and Irony in the New Testament: Illuminated by Parallels in Talmud and Midrash*. Reykjavik: Bokautgafa Menningarsjods, 1965.

Kenner, Hugh. *Mazes: Essays*. San Francisco: North Point, 1989.

Kierkegaard, Søren. *Fear and Trembling*. Garden City, NY: Doubleday, 1955.

Kirkpatrick, A. F. *The Book of Psalms*. Cambridge: Cambridge University Press, 1902.

Knox, Ronald A. *Essays in Satire*. London: Sheed and Ward, 1930.

Kolakowski, Leszek. *Tales from the Kingdom of Lailonia and the Key to Heaven*. Chicago: University of Chicago Press, 1989.

Kynes, Will. "Beat Your Parodies into Swords, and Your Parodied Books in Spears: New Paradigms for Parody in the Hebrew Bible." *Biblical Interpretation* 19 (2011) 276–310.

Lash, Nicholas. "Ministry of the Word or Comedy and Philology." *New Blackfriars* 68 (1987) 472–83.

Leibowitz, Nahama. *Studies in Bamidbar*. Translated and adapted by Aryeh Newman. Jerusalem: World Zionist Organization, 1980.

Lewis, C. S. *An Experiment in Criticism*, Cambridge: Cambridge University Press, 1962.

———. *Prince Caspian: The Return to Narnia*. New York: Collier, 1978.

———. *The Screwtape Letters and Screwtape Proposes a Toast*. Macmillan, 1970.

———. *Studies in Words*. 2nd ed. Cambridge: Cambridge University Press, 1967.

Lindvall, Terry. *God Mocks: A History of Religious Satire from the Hebrew Prophets to Stephen Colbert*. New York: New York University Press, 2015.

Longenecker, Bruce W. "A Humorous Jesus? Orality, Structure and Characterization in Luke 14:15–24, and Beyond." *Biblical Interpretation* 16 (2008) 179–204.

Lowell, James Russell. "Humor, Wit, Fun, and Satire." In *The Function of a Poet and Other Essays*. New York: Houghton Mifflin, 1920.

Luther, Martin. *Minor Prophets I: Hosea–Malachi*. Luther's Works 18. Edited by Jaroslav Pelikan. Saint Louis: Concordia, 1975.

———. *Selected Psalms I*. Luther's Works 12. Edited by Jaroslav Pelikan. Saint Louis: Concordia, 1955.

MacDonald, George. "The Wise Woman." In *Evenor*, 115. New York: Ballantine, 1972.

Magonet, Jonathan. *Form and Meaning: Studies in Literary Techniques in the Book of Jonah*. Sheffield: Sheffield Academic, 1983.

———. "Jonah, Book of." *Anchor Bible Dictionary*, 3:936–42. New Haven: Yale University Press, 1992.

Manson, T. W. *The Servant Messiah*. Cambridge: Cambridge University Press, 1961.

Marcus, Joel. *Mark 1–8*. Anchor Bible 27. New York: Doubleday, 1999.

———. *Mark 8–16*. Anchor Bible 27B. New Haven: Yale University Press, 2009.

Martinich, Mike W. "A Theory of Communication and the Depth of Humor." *Journal of Literary Semantics* 10 (1981) 20–31.

McCall Smith, Alexander. *The Comforts of a Muddy Saturday*. New York: Anchor, 2009.

McCleod, Mark S. "Making God Dance: Postmodern Theorizing and the Christian College." *Christian Scholar's Review* 21 (1992) 275–92.

McKane, William. *Jeremiah: Volume I*. International Critical Commentary on the Holy Scriptures. Edinburgh: T. & T. Clark, 2000.

———. "Observations on the *Tikunne*." In *On Language, Culture, and Religion: In Honor of Eugene Nida*, edited by Matthew Black and William A. Smalley, 53–77. The Hauge: Mouton, 1974.

———. *Proverbs*. 2nd ed. Philadelphia: Westminster, 1975.

Miles, Jack. "Laughing at the Bible: Jonah as Parody." *Jewish Quarterly Review* 65 (1974–1975) 169–81.

Miller, Patrick. "The Blessing of God: An Interpretation of Numbers 6:22–27." *Interpretation* 29 (1975) 240–51.

Moberly, R. W. L. *The Bible, Theology, and Faith: A Study of Abraham and Jesus*. Cambridge: Cambridge University Press, 2000.

———. *Old Testament Theology: Reading the Hebrew Bible as Christian Scripture*. Grand Rapids: Baker Academic, 2013.

Monro, D. H. *Argument of Laughter*. Notre Dame: University of Notre Dame Press, 1963.

Morley, Christopher. *The Haunted Bookshop*. Philadelphia: Lippincott, 1955.

Morreal, John, ed. *The Philosophy of Laughter and Humor*. Albany, NY: State University of New York Press, 1987.

Mulkay, Michael. *On Humor: Its Nature and Its Place in Modern Society*. Oxford: Blackwell, 1988.

Murdoch, Iris. *Metaphysics as a Guide to Morals*. London: Penguin, 1994.

Nash, Walter. *The Language of Humour: Style and Technic in Comic Discourse*. London: Longman, 1985.

Nemerov, Howard. *Bottom's Dream: The Likeness of Poems to Jokes*. New Brunswick, NJ: Rutgers University Press, 1972.

Niebuhr, Reinhold. "Humour and Faith." In *The Essential Reinhold Niebuhr*, edited by Robert McAfee Brown, 49–60. New Haven: Yale University Press, 1987.

Obrdlik, Antonin J. "'Gallows Humor'—A Sociological Phenomenon." *The American Journal of Sociology* 47 (1941–42) 709–16.

Palmer, Jerry. *The Logic of the Absurd: On Film and Television Comedy*. London: British Film Institute, 1987.

Peterson, Eugene H. *First and Second Samuel*. Louisville: Westminster John Knox, 1999.

———. *The Message: The Bible in Contemporary Language*. Colorado Springs: Navpress, 2002.

———. *Reversed Thunder: The Revelation of John and the Praying Imagination*. San Francisco: HarperOne, 1991.

———. *Under the Unpredictable Plant: An Exploration in Vocational Holiness*. Grand Rapids: Eerdmans, 1992.

Petrotta, Anthony J. *Lexis Ludens: Wordplay and the Book of Micah*. American University Studies Series 7, vol. 105. New York: Lang, 1991.

———. "Test of Balaam: Locating Humor in a Biblical Text." In *Probing the Frontiers of Biblical Studies*, edited by J. Harold Ellens and John T. Greene, 280–300. Eugene, OR: Pickwick, 2009.

———. "The Ways We Read." *Radix* 36:4 (2012) 4–9.

Phillips, Adam. "'What's So Funny?' On Being Laughed At . . ." In *The Anatomy of Laughter*, edited by Toby Garfitt et al., 124–30. London: Legenda, 2005.

Propp, Vladimir. *On the Comic and Laughter*. Translated by Jean-Patrick Debbèche and Paul J. Perron. Toronto Studies in Semiotics and Communication. Toronto: University of Toronto Press, 2009.

Radday, Yehuda Thomas, and Athalya Brenner. *On Humor and the Comic in the Hebrew Bible*. Sheffield: Almond, 1990.

Rahner, Hugo. *Man at Play*. 1972. Reprint, Eugene, OR: Wipf & Stock, 2001.

Ramban. *Ramban on Genesis*. https://www.sefaria.org/Ramban_on_Genesis.18.14?lang=bi.

Ross, Herbert, dir. *The Sunshine Boys*. 1 hour 51 min. United Artists, 1975.

Sanders, Barry. *Sudden Glory: Laughter as Subversive History*. Boston: Beacon, 1995.

Sarna, Nahum M. *Genesis: The Traditional Text with New Jewish Publication Society Translation and Commentary*. Philadelphia: Jewish Publication Society, 1989.

Sasson, Jack M. *Jonah*. Anchor Bible 24B. New York: Doubleday, 1990.

Sayers, Dorothy L., trans. and ed. *The Comedy of Dante Alighieri: Purgatory. Vol 2*. Middlesex: Penguin, 1955.

Screech, M. A. *Laughter at the Foot of the Cross*. Boulder, CO: Westview, 1999.

Shakespeare, William. *A Midsummer Night's Dream*. The Riverside Shakespeare. Boston: Houghton Mifflin, 1974.

Shapiro, David. "Proverbs." In *Congregation, Contemporary Writers Read the Jewish Bible*, edited by David Rosenberg, 313–30. New York: Harcourt Brace Jovanovich, 1987.

Shemesh, Abraham Ofir. "The Rabbis Maintained It Was Flaxseed." *Biblical Theology Bulletin* 49:3 (2019) 156–67.

Skinner, John. *A Critical and Exegetical Commentary on Genesis*. International Critical Commentary on the Old and New Testaments. 2nd ed. T. & T. Clark, 1969.

Slavitt, David R. *Sixty-One Psalms of David*. Oxford: Oxford University Press, 1996.

Smith, A. J. *Metaphysical Wit*. Cambridge: Cambridge University Press, 1991.

Strawn, Brent A. "On Vomiting: Leviticus, Jonah, and Ea(a)rth." *Catholic Biblical Quarterly* 74 (2012) 452–59.

Stone, Robert. *Damascus Gate*. New York: Touchstone, 1998.

Story, G. M., and Helen Gardner, eds. *The Sonnets of William Alabaster*. London: Oxford University Press, 1959.

Swabey, Marie Collins. *Comic Laughter: A Philosophical Essay*. Handen: Archon, 1970.

Taplin, Oliver, and Maurice Platnauer. "Aristophanes." https://www.britannica.com/biography/Aristophanes.

Thiselton, Anthony. *New Horizons in Hermeneutics: The Theory and Practice of Transforming Biblical Reading*. Grand Rapids: Michigan, 1992.

Tolkien, J. R. R. *The Letters of J. R. R. Tolkien*. Boston: Houghton Mifflin, 1981.

Tomko, Helena M. "A Good Laugh Is Hard to Find: From Destructive Satire to Sacramental Humor in Evelyn Waugh's *Helena*." *Christianity & Literature* 67:2 (2018) 312–31.

Ullendorf, Edward. "The Bawdy Bible." *Bulletin of the School of Oriental and African Studies* 42:3 (1979) 425–56.

van Harn, Roger E., and Brent A. Strawn, eds. *Psalms for Preaching and Worship: A Lectionary Commentary*. Grand Rapids: Eerdmans, 2009.

von Rad, Gerhard. *Genesis: A Commentary*. Old Testament Library. Philadelphia: Westminster, 1961.

Waldock, A. J. A. *Paradise Lost and Its Critics*. Cambridge: Cambridge University Press, 1961.

Wat, Aleksander. *Lucifer Unemployed*. Evanston, IL: Northwestern University Press, 1990.

Wells, Samuel (and George Sumner). *Esther & Daniel*. Grand Rapids: Brazos, 2013.

———. *Improvisation: The Drama of Christian Ethics*. Grand Rapids: Brazos, 2004.

Weiser, Artur. *Psalms: A Commentary*. Philadelphia: Westminster, 1962.

Whedbee, J. William. *The Bible and the Comic Vision*. Cambridge: Cambridge University Press, 1998.

Williams, D. H., trans. and ed. *Matthew: Interpreted by Early Christian Commentators*. Grand Rapids: Eerdmans, 2018.

Williams, James G. "The Power of Form: A Study of Biblical Proverbs." *Semeia* 17 (1980) 35–58.

Williams, Rowan. *The Tragic Imagination*. Oxford: Oxford University Press, 2016.

Wilson, A. N. *The Vicar of Sorrows*. New York: Norton, 1993.

Wisse, Ruth. *No Joke: Making Jewish Humor*. Princeton: Princeton University Press, 2013.

Wolff, Hans. *Obadiah and Jonah*. Philadelphia: Fortress, 1991.

Wood, Ralph. *Flannery O'Connor and the Christ-Haunted South*. Grand Rapids: Eerdmans, 2004.

Zinnemann, Fred, dir. *A Man for All Seasons*. 2 hours. Columbia Pictures, 1966.

Zlotowitz, Meir, and Nosson Scherman. *Jonah / Yonah: A New Translation With a Commentary Anthologized from Talmudic, Midrashic and Rabbinic Sources*. 2nd ed. New York: Mesorah, 1980.